THE SQUARE AND THE CIRCLE

THE SQUARE AND THE CIRCLE

*The Influences of Freemasonry
on Wicca and Paganism*

BY PAYAM NABARZ

Published by Avalonia

www.avaloniabooks.co.uk

Published by Avalonia
BM Avalonia, London, WC1N 3XX, England, UK
www.avaloniabooks.co.uk

THE SQUARE AND THE CIRCLE
© Payam Nabarz, 2015
All rights reserved.

First published by Avalonia, May 2016
ISBN 978-1-905297-81-8

Typesetting and design by Satori
Illustrations as credited in the text.

British Library Cataloguing in Publication Data. A catalogue record for this book is available from the British Library.

Payam Nabarz is author of *The Mysteries of Mithras: The Pagan Belief That Shaped the Christian World* (Inner Traditions, 2005), *The Persian Mar Nameh: The Zoroastrian Book of the Snake Omens & Calendar* (Twin Serpents, 2006), and *Divine Comedy of Neophyte Corax and Goddess Morrigan* (Web of Wyrd Press, 2008). He is also the editor of *Mithras Reader: An academic and religious journal of Greek, Roman, and Persian Studies*. Volume 1 (2006), Volume 2 (2008), and Volume 3 (2010). His latest books are *Stellar Magic: A Practical Guide to Rites of the Moon, Planets, Stars and Constellations* (Avalonia, 2009); *Seething Cauldron: Essays on Zoroastrianism, Sufism, Freemasonry, Wicca, Druidry, and Thelema* (Web of Wyrd Press, 2010); and *Anahita: Persian Goddess and Zoroastrian Yazata* (Avalonia, 2013).

Persian-born Payam Nabarz is a Sufi and a Dervish. He is a Druid in the Order of Bards, Ovates and Druids, and a co-founder of its Nemeton of the Stars Grove. Magi Nabarz is a revivalist of the Temple of Mithras, a Hierophant in the Fellowship of Isis, a Past Master in the Craft (Freemasonry) and a Companion in the Royal Arch. He has also worked with the Golden Dawn system, Thelema, Nath Tantra, and Wicca. He was the founder of Spirit of Peace, a charitable organisation dedicated to personal inner peace and world peace via interfaith dialogue between different spiritual paths. His other interests include cycling and learning Yoga and Tai Chi.

Dedicated to my family.

ACKNOWLEDGMENTS

I would like to thank Hannah Fox and Graham King at the Museum of Witchcraft, Boscastle, Cornwall for their help with material shown in Figure: 2 and Figure: 3.

I would like to thank Mogg Morgan, Ric Lovett, and Akashnath for their overall helpful discussions, and Jack Daw, Michael Clarke, Julia Pissano, for their helpful comments on the Traditional Witchcraft chapter.

I would like to thank the members of the University of Edinburgh Lodge for their support and inspiring discussions on Freemasonry.

I would like to thank Alison Jones for reading this manuscript and her helpful comments, and Sacred Texts (sacred-texts.com) for making their resources available.

This book is a revised and expanded edition of an earlier version published as an essay in the Seething Cauldron in 2010.

Note: This book discusses several mystery schools, such as Freemasonry, Wicca, and Sufism; all of which have their own 'secrets'. Freemasonry is not a secret society, but a society with secrets, though the only actual secrets are "the traditional words and signs of recognition used as proof of membership" [1] . That is to say, the only secrets in Freemasonry are the sign, the grip and the token, which the United Grand Lodge of England confirms as secrets of the degree.[2] These secrets shall remain secret here too, and all confidences are kept: everything discussed in this book on Freemasonry is information publically available from the Freemasons' Library and Museum, London, or material from the Freemasons' Hall Museum shop. The material on Wicca, Sufism and other systems included here are also publically available to all researchers, and no confidential secrets are revealed.

---

1 The History of English Freemasonry, John Hamill, Lewis Masonic, 1994, p158.
2 Turning the Hiram Key: Making Darkness Visible, by Robert Lomas, 2007, p65.

Thou shalt find to the left of the House of Hades a spring,
And by the side thereof standing a white cypress.
To this spring approach not near.
But thou shalt find another, from the Lake of Memory
Cold water flowing forth, and there are guardians before it.
Say, 'I am a child of Earth and starry Heaven;
But my race is of Heaven (alone). This ye know yourselves.
But I am parched with thirst, and I perish. Give me quickly
The cold water flowing forth from the Lake of Memory.'
And of themselves they will give thee to drink of the holy
spring-
And thereafter among the other heroes thou shalt have
lordship.

-The Funerary Gold Plate from Petelia, South Italy,
3-4th century. B.C.

Mircea Eliade, *From Primitives to Zen: The Initiates In The*
Orphic-Pythagorean Brotherhood,
translation William Keith Chambers Guthrie, *Orpheus and*
Greek Religion (London, 1935), pp. 172-3

CONTENTS

INTRODUCTION

'Shall the folly of idiots, and the malice of the scornful, so much prevail that he who seeketh no worldly gain or glory at their hands...but only for God the treasure of heavenly wisdom and knowledge....be condemned as a companion of hellhounds, and a caller, and conjuror of wicked and damned spirits?'

- Dr. John Dee, Mathematical Praeface

'She is more precious than all riches: and all the things that are desired, are not to be compared to her. Length of days is in her right hand, and in her left hand riches and glory. Her ways are beautiful ways, and all her paths are peaceable. She is a tree of life to them that lay hold on her: and he that shall retain her is blessed. The Lord by wisdom hath founded the earth; hath established the heavens by prudence. By his wisdom, the depths have broken out, and the clouds grow thick with dew.'

- Book of Proverbs 3:15-20 and part of Royal Arch Freemasonry.

Wicca and Freemasonry - on the face of it nothing could be further apart: Wicca is a Goddess/God-centric Neo-Pagan mystery school, whose Rede is *'An it harm none, do what ye Will'*; while Freemasonry is a brotherhood/sisterhood and system of morality veiled in allegory, taught in a symbolic language, whose great principles are brotherly love, relief and truth. However, as we delve deeper, the level of influence of Freemasonry on Wicca becomes apparent. This is of social and anthropological significance, as Wicca perhaps is the only religion and mystery school that was born in Britain in the 20th Century, as well as exported to other countries. It has been growing rapidly in the rest of the world ever since. Wicca is one of fastest growing religions in the UK and the US. In the US one poll in the year 2000 estimated the number of Wiccan and Neo-Pagans as 768,400. In the 2001 UK national census, there were nearly 80,000 pagans (Wiccans, Druids, etc.) making it the seventh largest religion in the UK, whilst the latest estimates are about five times that number (400,000). For example, the summer solstice celebration at Stonehenge is attracting more and more people each year (35,000 in 2009). In the 2001 census seven in 10,000 UK respondents identified as Pagan; this number doubled in the 2011 census to fourteen in 10,000 respondents.

Freemasonry is a worldwide phenomenon, with lodges in many countries; most countries have their own Grand Lodges. However, Freemasonry was banned in the Soviet Union during the Communist era and was banned in Nazi Germany. Modern day Freemasons remember the Freemasons persecuted by the Nazi regime, and others, by wearing a blue forget-me-not flower lapel pin (Figure: 1). According to Masonic myth, during the Nazi reign, some Freemasons in Germany wore the blue flower lapel pin as means of identifying each other. The first formal interdiction of Freemasonry in Germany took place in August 1935, and many Freemasons ended their lives in the concentration camps [3], despite all Freemasonry lodges reforming themselves to comply with the new German government, except one that dissolved itself rather than

---

3 25 years of Freemasonry in Eastern Europe, Peter Hoffer, The Square magazine, December 2014, p65.

conform[4]. Freemasonry is still banned in most Arab and Islamic countries where it is deemed as a Western Imperialist organisation or a Zionist conspiracy: Freemasons have even been targeted by radical Islamic groups and terrorists. The Catholic Church between 1738 to 1974 'forbade Catholics to join the Freemasons or any similar organisation under pain of excommunication'[5]. The fact that both Wicca and Freemasonry are viewed suspiciously by many people is one of the elements that they have in common.

Figure 1 - Modern-day Freemasons remember the Freemasons persecuted by Nazi Germany and others by wearing a blue Forget-Me-Not flower lapel pin (Photo: by Payam Nabarz).

In the United Kingdom, Freemasonry has not technically been a secret society since the 1799 Unlawful Societies Act, when all secret societies became illegal. Freemasonry ceased to be a 'secret society' at that time, and was allowed to continue only

---

4 United Grand Lodge and United Grand Lodges of Germany 1946-1961, Alain Bernheim,Ars Quatuor Coronatorum, Vol 127 2014, p66.
5 The History of English Freemasonry, John Hamill, Lewis Masonic, 1994, p160.

by all lodges annually handing over to the local Clerk of the Peace the names of all their members together with their occupations and addresses[6]; this continued until the major criminal law reforms of the 1967 Criminal Justice Act. Freemasonry is not a secret society, but a society with secrets, though the only actual secrets 'are the traditional words and signs of recognition used as proof of membership'[7]: everything else, such as the details of Masonic ceremonies, ritual clothing, Temple designs, Officers' Jewels, book of Constitutions and Regulations, meeting venues etc... are all publicly available. This may come as a surprise to many people.

Freemasonry expanded hugely in the 1900s, reaching its peak in the 1950s; current numbers are a significant drop from their twentieth-century peak. In the US in 1959 there were over 4 million Freemasons, this was down to just over 1.2 million in 2014[8].

In the UK, under the United Grand Lodge of England, there are over 250,000 Freemasons. There are Grand Lodges in Ireland (which covers both Northern Ireland and Eire) and Scotland which have a combined total of approximately 150,000 members. Worldwide, there are approximately 6 million Freemasons[9]. One Freemason writer describes this situation as follows: 'Lower membership numbers are a fact of life. Ever since the 1970s and the near-total inability of the Craft to attract the "lost generation" of baby boomers (sons of

---

6 ibid, p56.
7 ibid, p158.
8 Masonic Service Association of North America Masonic Membership Statistics: www.msana.com/msastats.asp.
9 United Grand Lodge of England official website www.ugle.org.uk/what-is-freemasonry/frequently-asked-questions

our older members, fathers of our younger members),
our membership curve has been heading for the
basement, with little or no recovery predicted'[10] Despite
the decline in Freemason membership the Freemason's
charity contributions in the UK are second only to
those of the National Lottery. The principles of
Freemasonry are brotherly love, relief and truth.
Freemasons are true to their word, and the relief or
charity contributions in the UK alone, via the Grand
Charity is very significant: 'During its first thirty years
the Freemasons' Grand Charity gave grants totalling
over £100 million, helping thousands of individuals
and hundreds of charities.'[11]

What I propose in this work is that the perception
of the general decline of interest in Freemasonry should
be re-examined in this light: while Freemasonry itself
might have been on a decline in the last few decades,
the various social and spiritual movements it has
influenced, such as Wicca, are on an increase.

There has been a plethora of academic research
into the origins of Neo-Paganism in last few years, and,
many of the perceived 'facts' about paganism have been
strongly challenged. The purpose of this book is to
review the published work on the history of Neo-
Paganism and examine the evidence in the context of
English Freemasonry.

---

10 www.masonicdictionary.com/dues2.html
11 www.grandcharity.org/pages/history.html

THE HERMETIC ORDER OF THE GOLDEN DAWN

My visit in 2009 to the to the world-renowned Museum of Witchcraft in Boscastle, Cornwall, England sparked the writing of this book. There an object caught my attention (Figure: 2). In the Hermetic Order of the Golden Dawn section of the museum, there is an original summons (invite) to Isis-Urania Lodge no 3 of the Golden Dawn. The summons is for members to attend a ceremony on 21st July 1894, which is from the early days of the Golden Dawn – which was founded circa 1888.

The venue of the meeting was the Freemasons' Hall in Queen Street, London. It is an interesting piece of history as it firmly demonstrates the link between the Golden Dawn and Freemasonry; the Golden Dawn founders were Freemasons and used to meet in the Halls. The Hermetic Order of the Golden Dawn was an occult and magical society founded in the late 19th century in England, whose three founders, William Robert Woodman, William Wynn Westcott, and Samuel Liddell MacGregor Mathers were all Freemasons and also members of the *Societas Rosicruciana in Anglia* (S.R.I.A.) which is a Freemason side order.

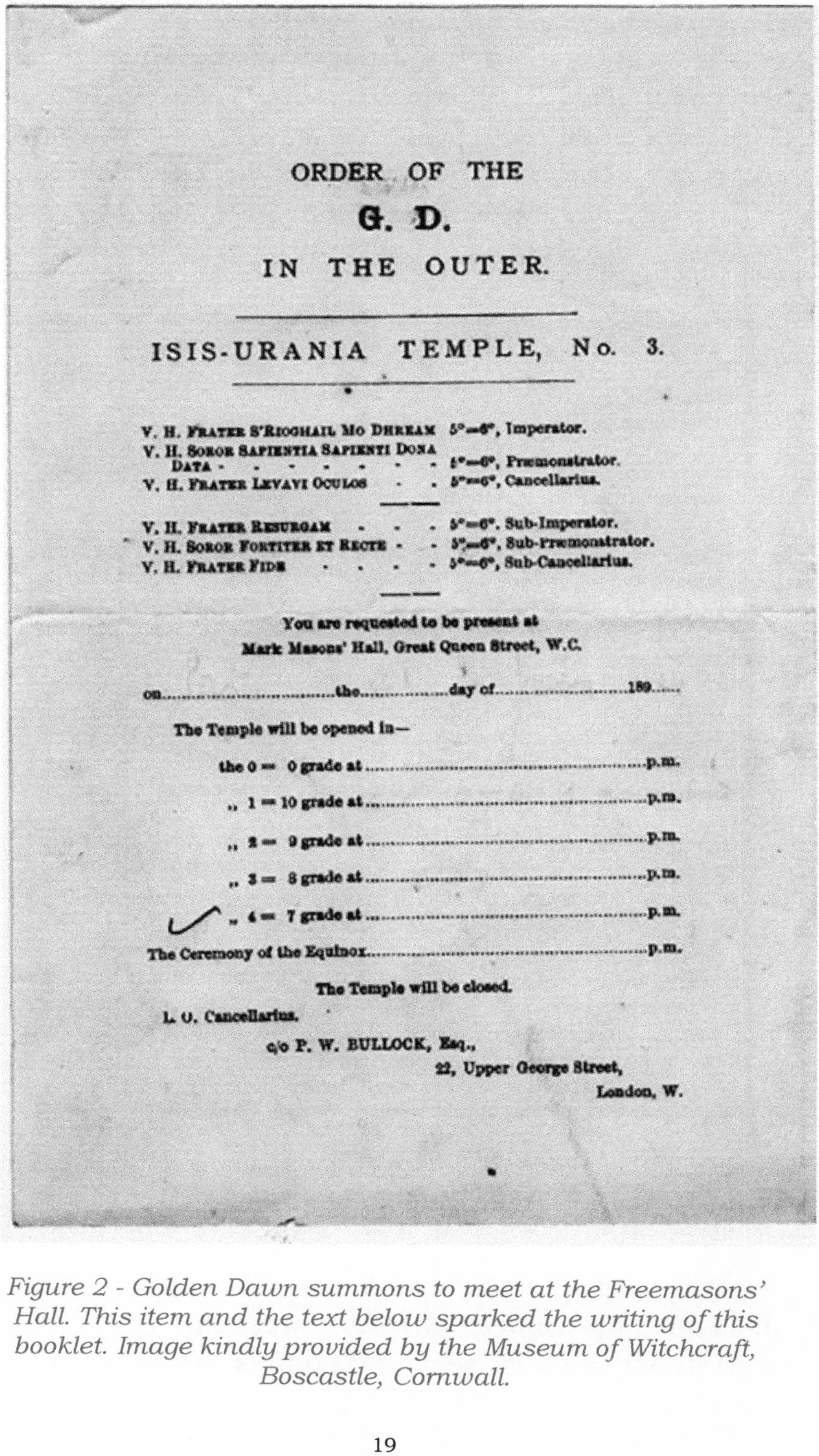

ORDER OF THE

G. D.

IN THE OUTER.

ISIS-URANIA TEMPLE, No. 3.

V. H. FRATER S'RIOGHAIL MO DHREAM	5°—6°, Imperator.
V. H. SOROR SAPIENTIA SAPIENTI DONA DATA	5°—6°, Præmonstrator.
V. H. FRATER LEVAVI OCULOS	5°—6°, Cancellarius.
V. H. FRATER RESURGAM	5°—6°, Sub-Imperator.
V. H. SOROR FORTITER ET RECTE	5°—6°, Sub-Præmonstrator.
V. H. FRATER FIDE	5°—6°, Sub-Cancellarius.

You are requested to be present at
Mark Masons' Hall, Great Queen Street, W.C.

on........................the................day of...................189......

The Temple will be opened in—

the 0 — 0 grade at ....p.m.

„ 1 — 10 grade at ....p.m.

„ 2 — 9 grade at ....p.m.

„ 3 — 8 grade at ....p.m.

„ 4 — 7 grade at ....p.m.

The Ceremony of the Equinox...p.m.

The Temple will be closed.

L. O. Cancellarius.

c/o P. W. BULLOCK, Esq.,
22, Upper George Street,
London, W.

Figure 2 - Golden Dawn summons to meet at the Freemasons' Hall. This item and the text below sparked the writing of this booklet. Image kindly provided by the Museum of Witchcraft, Boscastle, Cornwall.

Another fascinating thing about this item was the details written about the artefact by the Museum of Witchcraft (Figure: 3), which reads: "There are many aspects of ritual and magic that link Freemasonry and witchcraft. The three degrees of Wiccan witchcraft involve rituals that are very similar to the Masonic degrees...."

 Freemasonry and Witchcraft

There are many aspects of ritual and magic that link Freemasonry and witchcraft.

The three degrees of Wiccan witchcraft involve rituals that are very similar to the Masonic degrees. The use of cords and a ritual death and resurrection are particularly striking examples.

Expressions like "So mote it be" are common to both Wiccan and Masonic ritual.

We are unable to elaborate on the similarities of ritual without betraying trust. Visitors wishing to study this link will find no shortage of publications on Masonic and Wiccan ritual.

Many of the symbols used by witches are also used by Freemasons - there is a large pentagram set into the floor in the entrance to Freemasons Hall. It was the Masons that carved the Greenmen and Sheela-na-gigs in churches.

The higher degrees of Freemasonry recall many of the ancient magical mystery cults including the Rose Croix, the Knights Templar and The Royal Arch. Mysteries from the "Key of Solomon" and the Qabalah are incorporated in Wiccan Ritual, Masonic Ritual and by The Golden Dawn.

Figure 3 - This text was written by the Museum of Witchcraft, in the Golden Dawn section of the Museum. Image kindly provided by the Museum of Witchcraft, Boscastle, Cornwall.

This sparked an interest in me to find out what the links are, and indeed why the Museum, which has been in operation for years, still thinks they need to be kept a secret.

The Muse of this Museum (a shrine of the Muses) inspired me to follow these breadcrumbs, and led to my visiting the Muse in the Freemasons' Museum in London. This book is the result.

The Pagan and Wiccan sources of my study are the works of Professor Ronald Hutton, Philip Heselton, Frederic Lamond, Aidan A. Kelly, David Rankine, Sorita d'Este, Michael Howard, and a number of other researchers of the history of modern Wicca and Paganism. A full bibliography is included at the end of this book.

In addition to these, the Freemasons' Museum and Library and bookshop (located in Great Queen Street, London) were also studied, as this is where the Hermetic Order of the Golden Dawn originally met, and this venue could perhaps be seen as the birthplace of many of the twentieth-century esoteric schools. It was within the hallowed walls of the Freemasons' Hall where the first rites of the Isis-Urania Lodge of the Golden Dawn were performed by its Master Mason founders. The current building is the third Temple on the site, built between 1927–1932; the second was built in c.1860 and first in 1776; hence, the rooms where the Golden Dawn met in the late 1800s no longer exist in their original form.

The precursor to the Golden Dawn was Societas Rosicruciana in Anglia (SRIA, the Rosicrucian Society of England) which was founded in 1865 by two Freemasons; with only Master Masons being allowed to join. There are nine grades in the SRIA: Zelator, Theoricus, Practicus, Philosophus, Adeptus Minor, Adeptus Major, Adeptus Exemptus, Magister and Magi.

The SRIA, which is still in operation[12] was founded on the basis of manuscripts that were allegedly discovered in the vaults of the Freemasons' Hall. There are now over 90 colleges around the world.[13]

One visual link between Freemasonry, Hermetic Order of the Golden Dawn and modern Paganism can see in form of Rider-Waite tarot deck first published in 1910 and one of the most popular Tarot packs of all time, it is still the number one best seller Tarot on Amazon. For example, in The High Priestess card the High Priestess sits between the masonic columns. The Wheel of Fortune and The World card contain the Royal Stars covered later in Appendix III. The author was Arthur Edward Waite, a member of Hermetic Order of the Golden Dawn, a Freemason and member of SRIA. This Tarot pack brings various esoteric elements together.

While there is much debate about sources of the SRIA and the Golden Dawn manuscripts and texts (they were probably all written in the late 1800s), one thing is clear: the Freemasons' Hall in Great Queen Street, London, where the initial rituals of the Golden Dawn took place, is one of the key physical locations where the modern occult and pagan revival began; a place which perhaps should be one of the modern occultist's 'pilgrimage' tour sites! In addition to its Grand Temple, it contains 23 temples currently in operation, each designed individually, each of which appears different to each other, with differing capacities.

---

12 For further info on the Societas Rosicruciana in Anglia see: www.sria.info/home/
13 Beyond the Craft, Keith B. Jackson, Lewis Masonic, 2012, p73.

When researching a topic, finding inspiration (referred to as Awen in the Welsh tradition), is akin to being hit by lightning. In other words, it is not guaranteed. This is where libraries and museums can help. They can be lightning rods for inspiration: just sitting in one, surrounded by the collective ideas and works of thousands of minds over centuries, focuses the mind and allows ideas flow through, like the drops of the inspiration of Awen, from the Cauldron of Cerridwen.

At the street entrance of the Library and the Freemasons' Museum at the Freemasons' Hall, a large pentagram decorates the floor (Figure 4), a symbol significant to many mystery schools including Wicca, Druidry, the Golden Dawn and Freemasonry. The pentagram is now the official religious icon of Wicca, and in the US, the military graves of fallen American Wiccan soldiers have a pentagram carved on their memorial stones, instead of a Christian cross.

It is with the image of the pentagram in mind we begin this work and enter the mysteries.

Figure 4 - On the pavement outside the Library and Freemasons' Museum at the Freemasons' Hall, London.

WHAT IS FREEMASONRY?

The answer given by every initiate to this question is that Freemasonry is 'a peculiar system of morality veiled in allegory and illustrated by symbols'[14]. The first English Freemason Grand Lodge was established on 24th June 1717, at a meeting between four Old Lodges in the Goose and Gridiron pub, in the Churchyard of St Paul's cathedral in London; and in 1723 its regulations and Book of Constitution were published[15,16]. The exact history of Freemasonry before 1717 is more difficult to ascertain; though we know that Elias Ashmole, founder of the Ashmolean Museum (one of my favourite museums), was initiated in 1646. Two texts of great importance to Masonry are the Regius Manuscript (MS) and the Cooke MS[17]. The Regius MS is said to be the oldest Masonic document in existence, c.1390, and is in the British Museum; the text makes interesting reading.[18] The Cooke MS is the second oldest MS and is dated c.1420; it is also publicly available to read.[19] The analysis of the origins of Freemasonry is beyond the scope of this book, for those interested the works of John Hamill are recommended, especially his *The*

---

14 Emulation Lodge of Improvement, Emulation Ritual, Lewis Masonic, 2007,p114.
15 Freemasonry A Celebration of the Craft, John Hamill, and Robert Gilbert, forward by HRH Duke of Kent, Angus Books, 2004, p27.
16 The History Of English Freemasonry, John Hamill, Lewis Masonic, 1994, p19.
17 Freemasonry A Celebration of the Craft, John Hamill, and Robert Gilbert, forward by HRH Duke of Kent, Angus Books, 2004, p181.
18 www.freemasons-freemasonry.com/regius.html
19 http://freemasonry.bcy.ca/texts/cooke.html

History Of English Freemasonry (Lewis Masonic,1994) and the recent article *The Confused Origins of Freemasonry* by David V. Barrett *The Square* magazine, December 2014, pp7-9. It should be noted throughout this book that when I refer to Freemasonry I am referring predominantly to English Freemasonry.

There are three degrees in English Freemasonry, these are:

- Initiation (first degree)
- Passing (second degree)
- Raising (third degree)

A person who has received these degrees is called respectively:

1. Initiate
2. Fellowcraft
3. Master Mason

It is usual that the Master Mason then takes on an officer role within the lodge. There are seven progressive offices:

1. Steward
2. Inner Guard
3. Junior Deacon
4. Senior Deacon
5. Junior Warden
6. Senior Warden
7. Worshipful Master

A new Master Mason ideally spends a year in each of the office roles, in the above order. Hence, it would take around seven years before becoming a Worshipful Master and sitting in the Chair of King Solomon. The lodge structure is that the principal officers are called:

- Worshipful Master
- Senior Warden
- Junior Warden

There are also four assistant officers:

- Senior Deacon
- Junior Deacon
- Inner Guard
- Tyler

There are also a number of non-progressive officer roles which are:

- Immediate Past Master
- Chaplain
- Treasurer
- Secretary
- Director of Ceremonies
- Almoner
- Charity Steward
- Assistant Secretary
- Assistant Director of Ceremonies
- Organist
- Mentor
- Tyler

All of whom, as their job titles suggest, fulfil a specific practical function within the lodge.

The roles of the seven ritual officers, plus the Tyler, are as follows:

- The Tyler is situated outside the door of the lodge, and is armed with a drawn sword, to stop intruders, and prepares the candidates to enter the lodge.

- The Inner Guard is placed at the entrance of the lodge, and receives the candidates and admits Masons.
- The Junior Deacon sits at the right of the Senior Warden, and carries the messages of the Worshipful Master from the Senior Warden to the Junior Warden.
- The Senior Deacon sits at the near right of the Worshipful Master, and carries the communications of the Worshipful Master to the Senior Warden.
- The Junior Warden sits in the south of the lodge, and represents the sun at its apex at midday.
- Senior Warden sits in the West of the lodge and represents the sunset.
- The Worshipful Master sits in the east of the lodge and represents the sunrise.
- The Treasurer and Secretary sit in the north of the lodge.

Therefore, all stations of the sun are marked within the Temple, and the Temple is in shape of a parallelopipedon (rectangular with the six faces rectangles) built facing the East, with the Temple door in the West (Figure 5):

Figure 5 - The Temple is built on East to West alignment. (Image credit: Virtual Lodge of Instruction the producers and Lewis Masonic the suppliers, 2014).

Table 1 summarises the various Officers and their roles. [20] Freemason lodges are hierarchical in their organisation, but are also highly democratic. The various offices are for one year only and members move on to a different role each year, allowing them to learn the different ritual material and gain experience in all offices. For example, members who are part of several lodges might be a Deacon in one lodge, a Worshipful Master in one, and the Secretary in another.

20
www.ugle.org.uk/images/files/Book_of_Constitutions_2014_online_-_Craft_plates_reduced_size.pdf

Officer	Jewel/Emblem	Role
Worshipful Master	The Square	Sits in the East. Elected annually, and installed in the Chair and in charge of the Lodge for the year. Their architectural symbol is the Ionic order (Wisdom), and represents King Solomon.
Senior Warden	The Level	Sits in the West. Assists in opening and closing of the Lodge and its rituals. Their architectural symbol is the Doric order (Strength) and represents Hiram King of Tyre.
Junior Warden	The Plumb Rule	Sits in the South. Assists in opening and closing of the Lodge and the rituals. Their architectural symbol is the Corinthian order (Beauty) and represents Hiram Abif.

Chaplain	A book on a triangle surmounting a glory	Recites the non-denominational prayer at ceremonies and at opening and closing of the Lodge. The open book, the Volume of Sacred Law, is one of the great emblematical lights in Freemasonry.
Treasurer	A key	Manages all the finances of the Lodge, such as dues and dining.
Secretary	Two pens in saltire, tied with a ribbon.	Manages all the administrations aspects of the Lodge and minutes all the meetings.
Director of Ceremonies	Two rods in saltire, tied by a ribbon.	Directs all the ceremonies and rehearsals in the Lodge, and directs members and visitors to their correct seats.
Almoner	A scrip-purse, upon which is a heart.	Looks after the welfare of the members and arranges help for members if needed, and keeps in contact with Lodge's widows and ill members.

Charity Steward	A Trowel.	Manages the Lodge's charity and fundraising, passing on donations to various national or international charities. The trowel cements acts of charity that unite society.
Lodge Mentor	Two chisels in saltire.	Looks after the new members and answers their many questions.
Senior Deacon	Dove and olive branch (in some very old lodges symbol for the Deacon used is Hermes/Mercury, the Messenger of the Gods).	Guides the candidate during the ceremonies and carries messages from the Worshipful Master to the Senior Warden. The carrying of messages is why the symbol of Hermes/Mercury was originally used, but it was then replaced by the Dove, the messenger of peace and finder of land after the Biblical Great Flood.
Junior Deacon	Dove and olive branch (in some very old lodges symbol for the Deacon used is Hermes/Mercury, the Messenger of the Gods).	Guides the candidate during the ceremonies and carries messages from the Senior Warden to the Junior Warden.

Assistant Director of Ceremonies	Two rods in saltire, surmounted by a bar bearing the word 'Assistant'.	Helps the Director of Ceremonies in conducting all the ceremonies.
Assistant Secretary	Two pens in saltire, surmounted by a bar bearing the word 'Assistant'.	Helps the secretary to manage all the administration aspects of the Lodge.
Inner Guard	Two swords in saltire.	Sits in the Temple within the entrance and admits masons on proof.
Steward	A cornucopia (horn of plenty) between the legs of a pair of compasses extended.	Helps at the Festive Board and keeps everyone's glasses filled with wine. In some Lodges also serves the food.
Tyler	A sword.	Is located outside of the Lodge's guards with a drawn sword, prepares the candidates for the ceremony, and lights the candles and sets up the Lodge before opening.

Immediate Past Master	The square and the diagram of the 47th proposition of the 1st Book of Euclid engraved on a silver plate, pendant within it (Figure: 6).	Previous years' Worshipful Master, sits next to current Worshipful Master and acts as the Immediate Past Master, providing support and guidance when needed.
Organist	A lyre.	Music is one of the seven Liberal arts and sciences and an important part of Freemasonry. The playing of music is to bring concord and harmony to the meetings.

Table 1: Roles of the Officers of the Lodge (within the United Grand Lodge of England)[21].

21 Rees, Julian, Ornaments Furniture and Jewels, Lewis Masonic, 2013.
Emulation Lodge of Improvement, Emulation Ritual, Lewis Masonic, 2007.
Redman,Graham, The Worshipful Master's Work Today (Emulation Pocket), Lewis Masonic, 2011.
Redman,Graham, The Warden's Work Today: With Notes for the Master Elect (Emulation Pocket), Lewis Masonic, 2011.
Redman,Graham, The Installing Master's Work Today: With Notes for the Immediate Past Master (Emulation Pocket), Lewis Masonic, 2011.

Figure 6 - An example of an Officer's collar. This is a Past Master's symbol, depicting the square and the diagram of the 47th proposition of the 1st Book of Euclid

All the Officer's Jewels/collars have much symbolic meaning associated with them. For example, the Past Master Jewel (Figure: 6) is the 47th proposition of the 1st Book of Euclid:

'by it we can prove that in a triangle, one of the angles of which is a right angle, the square of the side opposite the right angle is equal to both the squares on the sides containing the right angle: it follows then that if we make any triangle in which the square of one side is equal to both the squares of the two other sides, then the angle opposite that side must be a true right angle—the angle of a correct square... In order to get a correct square angle it is therefore only necessary to make a triangle the sides of which are in the proportion 3-4-5. In connection with this, it is of much interest to know that as the standard and symbol of perfection with Speculative Masons now is the Square, so this right-angled triangle, which is almost identical, was with the Egyptians several thousand years ago as their standard and symbol of perfection; and they made it also the basis of all their measurements; looking upon it as the symbol of Universal Nature, the side with length 4 being Osiris the male principle, side length 3 the female principle Isis, and side length 5 Horus the son, the product of these two principles;—they further said that 3 was the first perfect odd number, that 4 was the square of 2 the first even number, and 5 was the sum of 3 and 2.'[22]

The basic Principles of Freemasonry for which the Grand Lodge of England has stood throughout its history are well documented and publically available. Some of these are:

---

22 Greene, Thomas Bro. The 47th Proposition, Ars Quatuor Coronatorum, Transactions of The Quatuor Coronati Lodge No. 2076 London.
www.freemasonry.bcy.ca/aqc/1901/euclid.html

"1. That a belief in the G.A.O.T.U. and His revealed will shall be an essential qualification for membership.

2. That all Initiates shall take their Obligation on or in full view of the open Volume of the Sacred Law, by which is meant the revelation from above which is binding on the conscience of the particular individual who is being initiated.

3. That the three Great Lights of Freemasonry (namely, the Volume of the Sacred Law, the Square, and the Compasses) shall always be exhibited when the Grand Lodge or its subordinate Lodges are at work, the chief of these being the Volume of the Sacred Law.

4. That the discussion of religion and politics within the Lodge shall be strictly prohibited etc..."[23]

The above describes the mechanics of the Lodge. However to capture the spirit of mystery schools, ancient or modern, in essay format is challenging, and is perhaps best expressed poetically. Therefore, to answer the questions "What is Freemasonry?" and "What is a Freemason's initiation?", I think the two poems below capture the spirit of it and subtly answer these questions. The first, written by the author, is called *'Initiate'*; the second is the classic poem by Rudyard Kipling (1865–1936) called *'The Mother Lodge'*:

---

23 www.ugle.org.uk/images/files/Information_Booklet_-_2014_-_online.pdf

INITIATE

Three candles lit,
Tyler's sword and curtain drawn,
Temple door locked.

Invisible pulleys and cogs turn,
as a Corinthian column-shaped lever is pulled down,
and an Ionic column-shaped lever handle is pushed up,
making traces of an ancient story visible on a board.

Knock, knock, knock!
Who seeks admission?
A traveller who seeks to quench their thirst for
knowledge,
stepping on the chequered path, with no trace of metal,
from darkness into the light,
life in balance pincered between a dagger and a cord.

The lesser lights illuminating the Temple,
the silver rays of the full moon, the golden rays of
summer solstice sun.
The Initiate walks sun-wise, marking the stations of the
sun in the cardinal directions:
saluting the dawn in the east, saluting the sun at its
meridian in the south,
saluting the sunset in the west, and silently passing the
sun at midnight in the north.

Ancient tongues and forgotten words,
given a new lease of life,
words echoed, sounds vibrated,
Creating a wave like a pebble in a lake,
reaching the shores of Great Temples long buried in the
sand.
A celestial music, timeless, boundless.

Mysteries revealed through experience,
steps taken on solid earth of a marble floor,
not absorbed via a TV screen.

The scroll of Doric column unrolled,
Cypher, Hieroglyphic, Cuneiforms, Oghams, Runes,
Wisdom, Beauty, Strength, unified.
Tapping the black and white pillars sounds hollow,
celestial globe and terrestrial globe,
on their apex, point to the secrets within.

Teachings of Euclid, Plato and Pythagoras recalled,
the seven liberal arts and sciences the syllabus.
Mobile phones, txt language, emoticons, celebrity culture,
politics, gossip, all opiums of the masses left at the door.
In the temple it is Grammar, Rhetoric, Logic, Arithmetic,
Geometry, Music, and Astronomy.
The elements centre stage, Fire Tetrahedron, Air
Octahedron, Earth Hexahedron, Water Icosahedron, and
the fifth element Universe Dodecahedron.

As above as below, turning the rough ashlar to a perfect
cube,
the seven Graces, like seven sisters of the Pleiades, your
guiding stars,
Their names thy daily mantra: Prudence, Justice,
Temperance, Fortitude, Faith, Hope, and Charity.
The metamorphosis en route to know thyself,
with Prometheus and Tubal Cain as thy travelling
companions.

The journey's end to die before you die,
staring into the skeletal reflection of your mortality
hovering above ground momentarily,

floating like a feather, suspended between heaven and
earth,
then lying in your cedar coffin, like Osiris awaiting
resurrection,
covered in earth, acacia and yew leaves,
brotherly midwives pulling you out of an earthly womb,
a new birth.
Now you are a candle maker,
darkness can be made visible, the abyss crossed,
the void bridged.

The sundial shows time has come to leave the Temple,
and return to the mundane world,
deosil procession out, and ritual gear laid down.

The ritual feast and toasts, a meal shared,
wine flowing, modernity and tradition hand in hand,
remembering absent friends at 9 o'clock.

The bar beckons, a circular shaped pint glass, on a
square beer mat.
We met sober and parted drunk.
What more is there to say widow's sons but,
Merry meet, merry part, and merry meet again.

by Payam Nabarz (13.6.14)

The poem *'The Mother Lodge'* by the Master Mason Rudyard Kipling is still valid today, as much as when he wrote it, as it demonstrates the universality of Freemasonry and its spirit. Kipling is perhaps best known for his *'The Jungle Book'* and poem *'IF';* interestingly his *'May Eve'* song is used in Wicca and is in the Wiccan Book of Shadows, and his *'A Song to Mithras'* is used in the Mithraic Neo-Pagan revival.

THE MOTHER LODGE

There was Rundle, Station Master,
An' Beazeley of the Rail,
An' 'Ackman, Commissariat,
An' Donkin' o' the Jail;
An' Blake, Conductor-Sargent,
Our Master twice was 'e,
With 'im that kept the Europe-shop,
Old Framjee Eduljee.

Outside -- "Sergeant! Sir! Salute! Salaam!"
Inside -- "Brother", an' it doesn't do no 'arm.
We met upon the Level an' we parted on the Square,

An' I was Junior Deacon in my Mother-Lodge out there!

We'd Bola Nath, Accountant,
An' Saul the Aden Jew,
An' Din Mohammed, draughtsman
Of the Survey Office too;
There was Babu Chuckerbutty,
An' Amir Singh the Sikh,
An' Castro from the fittin'-sheds,
The Roman Catholick!

We 'adn't good regalia,
An' our Lodge was old an' bare,
But we knew the Ancient Landmarks,
An' we kep' 'em to a hair;
An' lookin' on it backwards
It often strikes me thus,
There ain't such things as infidels,
Excep', per'aps, it's us.

For monthly, after Labour,
We'd all sit down and smoke
(We dursn't give no banquits,
Lest a Brother's caste were broke),
An' man on man got talkin'
Religion an' the rest,
An' every man comparin'
Of the God 'e knew the best.

So man on man got talkin',
An' not a Brother stirred
Till mornin' waked the parrots
An' that dam' brain-fever-bird;
We'd say 'twas 'ighly curious,
An' we'd all ride 'ome to bed,
With Mo'ammed, God, an' Shiv'
Changin' pickets in our 'ead.

Full oft on Guv'ment service
This rovin' foot 'ath pressed,
An' bore fraternal greetin's
To the Lodges east an' west,

Accordin' as commanded
From Kohat to Singapore,
But I wish that I might see them
In my Mother-Lodge once more!

I wish that I might see them,
My Brethren black an' brown,
With the trichies smellin' pleasant
An' the hog-darn passin' down; [Cigar-lighter.]
An' the old khansamah snorin' [Butler.]
On the bottle-khana floor, [Pantry.]
Like a Master in good standing
With my Mother-Lodge once more!

Outside -- "Sergeant! Sir! Salute! Salaam!"
Inside -- "Brother", an' it doesn't do no 'arm.
We met upon the Level an' we parted on the Square,
An' I was Junior Deacon in my Mother-Lodge out there![24]

This spirit of universal brotherhood of humans travelled to all its lodges as it spread across the globe. For example, in India, 'Provincial Grand Lodges were established in Bengal in 1729, Bombay in 1764, Madras in 1767, the Punjab in 1868, Northern India in 1951 and Ceylon (Shri Lanka) in 1810'[25], with the first Indian initiated in 1775. It was in these Indian Lodges that Rudyard Kipling and Gerald Gardner were initiated into Freemasonry, Rudyard Kipling in 1885, into the Hope and Perseverance Lodge No. 782 in Lahore, and Gerald Gardner in 1910, into the Sphinx Lodge in Colombo[26]. Rudyard Kipling wrote to The

24 For further info see: Rudyard Kipling and his Masonic Career www.freemasons-freemasonry.com/kipling.html
25 The History of English Freemasonry, John Hamill, Lewis Masonic, 1994, p99.
26 Modern Wicca: A History From Gerald Gardner to the Present, Llewellyn, Michael Howard, 2010, pp12-13.

Times, *'I was Secretary for some years of the Lodge...,
which included Brethren of at least four creeds. I was
entered [as an Apprentice] by a member from Brahmo
Somaj, a Hindu, passed [to the degree of Fellow Craft]
by a Mohammedan, and raised [to the degree of Master
Mason] by an Englishman. Our Tyler was an Indian
Jew.'* [27] In recent decades, multiculturalism is seen as a
recent left socialist agenda, yet this enlightened
approach has been an established part of Freemasonry
for over 200 years.

---

27 en.wikipedia.org/wiki/Rudyard_Kipling#Freemasonry

WHAT ARE WICCA AND PAGANISM?

If this question was posed to ten different Pagans, there would be twenty different answers. There are no central governing bodies in Neo-Paganism. There are networks, many orders, and organisations such as the Pagan Federation[28], but there is no overall governing body or doctrinally definitive Pagan creed which all Neo-Pagans agree on. I was a regional coordinator for the Pagan Federation for several years, and the topic of core principles was one that was discussed on a frequent basis. There are three principles which are a condition of membership when joining the Pagan Federation[29]:

- *Love for and Kinship with Nature. Reverence for the life force and its ever-renewing cycles of life and death.*
- *A positive morality, in which the individual is responsible for the discovery and development of their true nature in harmony with the outer world and community. This is often expressed as 'Do what you will, as long as it harms none'.*
- *Recognition of the Divine, which transcends gender, acknowledging both the female and male aspect of Deity.*

Essentially, all Neo-Pagan orders and groups only represent themselves and not the whole of Neo-Paganism. The majority of Neo-Pagans are non-

28 www.paganfed.org
29 www.paganfed.org/cms/index.php/federation/the-three-principles

conformist, left wing politically; though there are also a very small number of right wing Neo-Pagans. This means that getting a consensus for a definition of what a Pagan is, is rather challenging.

There are many different groups, with different training and initiatory structures. Neo-Pagans could be working solo or in groups, the groups could be a Coven, Seed group, Grove, Lodge, Iseums, Lyceums, etc. A three-degree structure is present in a number of systems: in some Wiccan groups the structure is: 1st degree (initiate), 2nd degree (Priest/Priestess), 3rd degree (High Priest/High Priestess); whilst in some Druid groups the three grades are Bard, Ovate, and Druid[30]. In the Fellowship of Isis, there are 33 Magi Degrees, the key three rites being first the Rite of Rebirth, then Ordination (becoming Priest/Priestess of the chosen deity), then Hierophancy (Hierophant)[31].

The 'Old English etymology for Witch gives us Wicca and *wicce*, with the plural *wiccan* for witches who practiced wiccecraeft'[32]. The word Pagan comes from Latin *Paganus,* which could mean country dweller, or refer to people living outside the Christian cities of the late Roman Empire. Paganism for the purposes here, and within the context of Europe, is best described as the religions of Europeans before the arrival of Christianity.

The situation is rather complex, as not all witches are pagans, some being Christians[33], who were also known to practice magic and witchcraft, especially in

---

30 www.druidry.org/
31 www.fellowshipofisis.com/mdegrees.html
32 Ameth: The Life and Times of Doreen Valiente by Jonathan Tapsell (Avalonia, 2014), p18.
33 Magic in the New Testament: A Survey and Appraisal of the Evidence by Robert Conner, Mandrake, 2010.

the early days of Christianity[34]. Some Christian use of magic and witchcraft into modern times is reported, as seen in the practice of dual observance, and some folk traditions.

Indeed, not all pagans are witches either, and in modern times, not all Wiccans are witches and not all witches are Wiccans. If we look back to ancient pagan societies and classical times, some pagans didn't practise witchcraft, and some forms of magic were deemed unlawful by the state Pagan clergy. According to the Museum of Witchcraft and Magic, the oldest laws on magic date to Plato's Laws (c. 348 BC) and to the ancient Babylonians, who differentiated between state-authorized and official magic practiced by the priests; and the magic practiced by sorcerers. This was also seen in the Greco-Roman world where magic practiced by followers of state Pagan religions were acceptable and seen as 'good magic', but the magic practiced by those who were a threat to the state and its law was deemed as 'bad magic'.

To summarise, European paganisms are the religions of indigenous Europeans, such religions as demonstrated by Celtic, Nordic, Greek, and Roman pantheons, etc., whose rites predate the advent of Christianity. Wicca is a modern branch of Neo-Paganism; there are many other branches, and most of the pre- Christian Pagan religions have been revived in recent history. Witchcraft can be described as a set of tools or techniques which can be used by Pagans, Christians, or members of any other religion. Therefore, it is important to distinguish Paganism, Wicca and Witchcraft for clarity. Wicca is also a mystery religion

---

34 Jesus the Sorcerer: Exorcist & Prophet of the Apocalypse by Robert Conner, Mandrake, 2006.

and as such it can be difficult to define and capture its true meaning.

The real spirit of Wicca is best captured in the concluding lines of the 1949 Wiccan 'Charge of the Goddess', also known as 'The Charge: Lift Up the Veil'.

THE CHARGE: LIFT UP THE VEIL

Magus: "Listen to the words of the Great Mother, who of old was also called among men Artemis, Astarte, Dione, Melusine, Aphrodite, Cerridwen, Diana, Arianrhod, Bride, and by many other names."

High Priestess: "At mine Altars the youth of Lacedaemon in Sparta made due sacrifice. Whenever ye have need of anything, once in the month, and better it be when the moon is full, ye shall assemble in some secret place and adore the spirit of Me who am Queen of all Witcheries and magics. There ye shall assemble, ye who are fain to learn all sorcery, yet have not won its deepest secrets. To these will I teach things that are yet unknown. And ye shall be free from slavery, and as a sign that ye be really free, ye shall be naked in your rites, both men and women, and ye shall dance, sing, feast, make music, and love, all in my praise. There is a Secret Door that I have made to establish the way to taste even on earth the elixir of immortality. Say, 'Let ecstasy be mine, and joy on earth even to me, to Me,' For I am a gracious Goddess. I give unimaginable joys on earth; certainty, not faith, while in life! And upon death, peace unutterable, rest, and ecstasy, nor do I demand aught in sacrifice."

Magus: "Hear ye the words of the Star Goddess."

High Priestess: "I love you: I yearn for you: pale or purple, veiled or voluptuous. I who am all pleasure, and purple and drunkenness of the innermost senses, desire you. Put on the wings, arouse the coiled splendour within you. Come unto me, for I am the flame that burns *in the heart of every man, and the core of every Star. Let it be your inmost divine self who art lost in the constant rapture of infinite joy. Let the rituals be rightly performed with joy and beauty. Remember that all acts of love and pleasure are my rituals. So let there be beauty and strength, leaping laughter, force and fire by within you. And if thou sayest, 'I have journeyed unto thee, and it availed me not,' rather shalt thou say, 'I called upon thee, and I waited patiently, and Lo, thou wast with me from the beginning,' for they that ever desired me shall ever attain me, even to the end of all desire.*[35]*

'The Charge: Lift Up the Veil' and parts of Wiccan degree material appear to be based partly on the Gnostic Mass and Book of the Law (*Liber AL vel Legis*) by Aleister Crowley. The most moving lines of chapter 1 of *Liber AL vel Legis* (from line 61 on) should be examined: the underlined section appears exactly in the Wiccan Charge. Line 61 reads: *'I charge you earnestly to come before me in a single robe, and covered with a rich head-dress. I love you! I yearn to you! Pale or purple, veiled or voluptuous, I who am all pleasure and purple, and drunkenness of the innermost sense, desire you. Put on the wings, and arouse the coiled splendour within you: come unto me! To me! To me!'*[36]

Other branches of modern Paganism use a wide range of historical materials from ancient Paganism, such the Orphic hymns, Egyptian texts, and other primary religious sources. Other related materials,

---

35 The Gardnerian Book of Shadows, by Gerald Gardner, at sacred-texts.com
36 *Liber AL vel Legis and Liber XV* by Aleister Crowley. www.sacred-texts.com/oto/engccxx.htm and www.sacred-texts.com/oto/lib15.htm

such as the Norse poetic Edda, or the Welsh poem the Mabinogion are also studied. Modern Paganism is a fertile land of both creativity and genuine historical research which enables those ancient religions to be revived.

The links between Freemasonry and the Neo-Pagan revival are not limited to Wicca, and in the Appendixes of this book we examine the links between Freemasonry and Druidry, Freemasonry and Traditional Witchcraft, and some related material of interest exploring links between Sufism and the Neo-Pagan revival.

THE ESOTERIC INTERSECTION

In the Venn diagram of the components of esoteric traditions, there are a number of overlaps or intersections between Freemasonry and other esoteric traditions, such as modern Wiccan and Neo-Pagan ones. These can be separated into three parts, which this chapter covers. Firstly, from the 1800s to the current time, some of the overlaps we see in modern Wiccan and Neo-Pagan practices are the direct result of the influence of Freemasonry on these groups in the 20th century onward. Secondly, if we look at the classical influences on Freemasonry some Pagan influence on Freemasonry is also observed, in that the works of ancient pagan philosophers such Euclid, Plato and Pythagoras are embedded in Freemasonry. The *Pythagorean Brotherhood* in a way is one of the inspirational ideals for Freemasonry. Thirdly, there are several areas of common ground between Freemasonry, Wicca, and Neo-Paganism, which are not necessarily influences one way or another, but are rather key components of Western esoteric traditions.

A ROUGH GUIDE TO PAGAN AND WICCAN HISTORY

In this chapter, a short summary of Wicca is presented as a Rough Guide to Neo-Paganism and Wiccan History. Turning the clock back to the late 19th and early 20th centuries, when Wicca and the Neo-Pagan movement began, some of the texts that influenced it were taken literally. For example, the anthropologist Margaret Murray's main work *'The Witch-Cult in Western Europe'*, published in 1921, had not yet stood the test of time; while Charles G. Leland's *'Aradia, Gospel of the Witches'*, translated and published in 1899, has many differences to the new 1999 version translated by Mario Pazzaglini. Furthermore, Leyland was paying his 'witch' source for more and more material, so encouraging her to come up with information. The mythology in Aradia is, of course, a pseudo-Christian one: for instance where it is stated in the book that Diana and the fallen angel Lucifer have a child together - Aradia, the first witch.

A towering figure in early twentieth century occultism was Aleister Crowley (1875–1947), whose great contribution was the philosophy of Thelema (Will), and who described himself as the 'Great Beast'! One wonders if Thelema became popular in the 1960s due to its message of doing whatever you want; (a misunderstanding of what its tenet of 'Do as thou Wilt' means), and again in the 1980s through the all-pervasive influence of counter-culture, such as Goth, Punk and Heavy Metal music, which picked up on some of its central themes. Although frowned upon by many, rebellious expressions remain deeply embedded in the music of youth culture, and reoccur in a cyclic manner as a cultural zeitgeist.

Crowley was one of the most influential characters in the Neo-Pagan revival, the remnants of his work can be seen in almost every Neo-Pagan tradition. However, some people are completely unaware that some of their material in fact comes from Crowley's writings. Crowley eventually also became the head of a quasi-Masonic order called *Ordo Templi Orientis* (O.T.O.) and was initiated into a number of irregular Freemason's Lodges. In one irregular lodge, in Mexico, he received the 33° in Scottish Rite Freemasonry (see Figure 7). He was also initiated into a lodge based in France, the Anglo-Saxon Lodge 343 (today numbered 103) which was incorporated under the French Masonic constitution in Paris. [37] The United Grand Lodge of England did not then recognise the French Grand Lodge, and as a result, Crowley was not recognised by any English regular lodges. Crowley described his not being recognised in detail in his autobiography:

'I returned to England some time later, after 'passing the chair' in my Lodge, and, wishing to join the Royal Arch, called on its venerable secretary.
I presented my credentials. '0 Thou Grand Architect of the Universe' the old man sobbed out in rage, 'why dost Thou not wither this impudent imposter with Thy fire from heaven? Sir, begone! You are not a Mason at all! As all the world knows, the people in Z- are atheists and live with other men's wives'.
I thought this a little hard on my Reverend Father in God my proposer; and I noted that, of course, every single English or American visitor to our Lodge in Z- stood in peril of instant and irrevocable expulsion on detection. So I said nothing, but walked to another room in Freemasons' Hall over his head, and took my seat as a Past Master in one of the oldest and most eminent Lodges in London!
Kindly note, furthermore, that when each of those wicked visitors returned to their Lodges after their crime, they automatically excommunicated the whole thereof; and as visiting is very common, it may well be doubted whether, on their showing, there is a single 'just, lawful and regular mason' left alive on the earth!' [38]

---

37 A Magick Life: a biography of Aleister Crowley by Martin Booth, Coronet Books, 2000, p303.
38 Confessions Of Aleister Crowley: An Autobiography by Aleister Crowley, edited by John Symonds & Kenneth Grant, published by Arkana books, (1989), p695.

While Crowley may not have been formally recognised, he states he attended a Lodge meeting taking his seat as a Past Master, which indicates that if the Junior Warden of that Lodge had done his job of testing new Visitors, Crowley knew all the passwords and signs to pass the examination by the Junior Warden of the Lodge.

To understand why Crowley was not recognised at this stage it is worth highlighting what a Masonic Order/Constitution is and what is the difference between regular and irregular Lodges are, as well as what "recognised" means. Freemason Lodges are supervised and governed at the regional level such as provincial or national borders by a Grand Lodge. All Grand Lodges have their own Constitution. For example, *The Book of Constitutions* is the rule book of the United Grand Lodge of England that regulates all English Lodges and Freemasons. The current edition, which includes all updates, is freely available for download from the internet, in four sections.[39]

Interactions between Grand Lodges are determined by the concept of Recognition. Each Grand Lodge maintains a list of other Grand Lodges which it recognises. Members of one Grand Lodge can only visit Lodges of the Grand Lodges their own Grand Lodge recognises, and visiting a Lodge of an unrecognised Grand Lodge is not allowed. The concept of Regularity is based on adherence to Masonic Landmarks, and the membership requirements and ideals of each Grand Lodge.

---

39 www.ugle.org.uk/about/book-of-constitutions

Figure 7 - Charter issued by Master Mason John Yarker, admitting Crowley to highest grade 33 degree of the Ancient and Accepted Scottish Rite of Masonry, dated 29th November, 1910.

For example, women Freemasons have two separate Grand Lodges in the UK, which are restricted to women and are deemed 'Regular' by the men-only United Grand Lodges of England (UGLE). However they cannot visit each other and are not recognised by each other.[40] Another recent example was in 2012, when the UGLE temporarily stopped recognising the National Grand Lodge of France (GLNF), which meant that UGLE and GLNF members could not visit each other's Lodges.[41] The other French Grand Lodge, the Grand Orient de France, and the United Grand Lodge of England (UGLE), have not recognised each other since 1877, with the UGLE deeming the Grand Orient de France as Irregular. This is why Crowley was not recognised as a 'regular' Mason by UGLE, and explains his 'joke' above of "it may well be doubted whether, on their showing, there is a single 'just, lawful and regular mason' left alive on the earth!"[42]

With regard to Crowley's Initiation (first degree), Passing (second degree) and Raising (third degree) in the Anglo-Saxon Lodge 343, according to Martin P. Starr in his paper *Aleister Crowley: Freemason!* (*Ares Quatuor Coronatorum*,1995): '*Crowley was initiated on 8 October 1904, presumably passed the following month, and raised on 17 December 1904; he is listed in the 'Tableau Annuel' dated 31 December 1904 with the Grand Lodge number 41210, Lodge number 54*'[43]. Perhaps more importantly and bringing us to the location of the Freemason's Hall London: '*Crowley's initiation into the grade of Neophyte of the Golden Dawn took place in the (Second) Mark Mason's Hall, Great*

---

40 www.hfaf.org/ugle.htm

41 http://freemasonrytoday.com/ugle-sgc/ugle/item/672-statements-on-grande-loge-nationale-francaise-glnf-withdrawal-of-recognition

42 Confessions Of Aleister Crowley: An Autobiography by Aleister Crowley, edited by John Symonds & Kenneth Grant, published by Arkana books, (1989), p696.

43 Aleister Crowley: freemason! by Bro. Martin P. Starr, 1995. Ars Quatuor Coronatorum, Transactions Of The Quatuor Coronati Lodge No. 2076 London.
www.freemasonry.bcy.ca/aqc/crowley.html

Queen Street, on 26 November 1898. In a real sense, this was Crowley's first distant brush with Freemasonry, as the Golden Dawn was created and led by an interlocking directorate of esoterically inclined Freemasons, with a ritual and organizational structure closely modelled on the Craft and certain Appendant Bodies. The parallels and blatant borrowings (e.g., the sceptres of the First and Third Principals in the Holy Royal Arch (a side order in Freemasonry) are used in the Golden Dawn rituals by the 'Hierophant' and 'Hegemon') which seem so obvious to a contemporary student...'[44]

There are photos of Aleister Crowley dressed in the regalia of a number of irregular Lodges - for example see Figure 8 and Figure 9; or plate 13b in the *Confessions Of Aleister Crowley.*[45] His Masonic credentials are further evidenced in the form of the Charter issued by Master Mason John Yarker, admitting him to highest grade 33 degree of the Ancient and Accepted Scottish Rite of Masonry: see plate 11 of the *Confessions Of Aleister Crowley.*[46] By taking into account the dates of his Initiation, Passing and Raising, all in 1904, and his receiving of the 33 degree Charter from John Yarker in 1910, it is clear Crowley ascended his masonic path very quickly indeed. To achieve this meteoric rise in six years (1904 to 1910) demonstrates he was focused and took his masonry as an important part of his path. Indeed, he states in his autobiography *'My association with Freemasonry was*

---

44 Aleister Crowley: freemason! by Bro. Martin P. Starr, 1995. Ars Quatuor Coronatorum, Transactions Of The Quatuor Coronati Lodge No. 2076 London.
www.freemasonry.bcy.ca/aqc/crowley.html
45 Confessions Of Aleister Crowley: An Autobiography by Aleister Crowley, edited by John Symonds & Kenneth Grant, published by Arkana books, (1989), p514.
46 ibid, p480.

therefore destined to be more fertile than almost any other study, and that in a way despite itself.'[47]

One of Crowley's creations was the Thoth Tarot pack, which was created working with Lady Frieda Harris (1877-1962). She was one of the executors of Crowley's Will, demonstrating how close they were. Her stylish drawings mean the Thoth Tarot pack is still one of most popular tarot designs amongst magicians and pagans today. Harris was also a member of the O.T.O. and a Freemason (Co-Mason), and her drawings included creating a set of Freemason Tracing Boards. Her three Entered Apprentice, Fellowcraft, and Master Mason Tracing Boards are masterpieces and in my view one of the best Freemason's Tracing Boards available.

Figure 8 - Aleister Crowley in his Ancient and Accepted Scottish Rite regalia 1912.

---

47 ibid, p708-709.

Figure 9 - Aleister Crowley in his full combined Masonic regalia 1916.

Crowley was not unique in his role of being both a Freemason and a magician. A less controversial but equally important figure in bridging the established Freemasonry and more esoteric path was William Wynn Westcott (1848-1925) who even has a *Societas Rosicruciana in Anglia* College (No. 11) named after him[48]. He was one of the founders of Hermetic Order of Golden Dawn, a coroner, scholar, translator, key member of the Theosophical Society, Master Mason and Worshipful Master of the Research Lodge Quatuor Coronati[49]. R. A. Gilbert's book on Westcott makes the

---

48 See details of College named after Westcott and still active www.sria.info/about-the-society/college-locations/united-kingdom/south-east-england-province/william-wynn-westcott-no-11/
49 Quatuor Coronati Lodge, No. 2076 is still active and

links between Freemasonry and the magical aspect clear through the various papers in the book: 'The Magical Mason: Forgotten Hermetic Writings of William Wynn Westcott, Physician and Magus'.[50] Furthermore, Westcott is perhaps one of the first authors who discusses the similarity between the Roman Pagan religion of the Cult of Mithras and Freemasonry in his paper 'The resemblances of Freemasonry to the Cult of Mithra.'[51] A subject which is close to my heart.

FREEMASONRY AND FOUNDERS OF WICCA

Gerald Brosseau Gardner (1884-1964) was the creator and founder of Wicca, and a visionary. He may have created Wicca because of his love for a certain lady [52] and naturism. However, he would deliberately play the trickster in order to popularize Wicca, which is no older than 100 years.

Gerald Gardner's link with Freemasonry goes back to his early life. When he was 25, he was initiated into Freemasonry in the 1900s[53]. Frederic Lamond states: *'Gerald had borrowed his initiation and circle opening ritual from Freemasonry and the Greater Key of Solomon to provide some atmosphere'*[54]. When Gerald Gardner met Crowley, on May Day of 1947, Crowley wrote in his diary that Gardner was a Royal Arch Freemason. [55]

---

thriving www.quatuorcoronati.com/
50 The Magical Mason: Forgotten Hermetic Writings of William Wynn Westcott, Physician and Magus (Roots of the Golden Dawn Series), by R. A. Gilbert, Aquarian Press(1983).
51 ibid, p244.
52 The Great Wicca Hoax - Part I, Adrian Bott, White Dragon Magazine, Lughnasa 2001.
53 Fifty Years of Wicca, Frederic Lamond, p9, p12. Green Magic, 2004.
54 ibid, p41.
55 Gerald Gardner & the Ordo Templi Orientis, by Rodney

However, Ronald Hutton in The Triumph of the Moon[56] seems uncertain if Gardner had in fact reached the very high grade of Royal Arch Freemason.

Crowley gave Gardner an Ordo Templi Orientis (O.T.O.) Charter for the 4th degree in 1947, and later same year raised him to the 7th degree. [57] Gardner apparently also paid Crowley for a subscription to the O.T.O. Charter. [58] While it may appear Gardner was fast-tracked through the O.T.O. by Crowley, it's worth remembering that originally Freemasons could join the O.T.O. at the degree level they already held.

If Crowley accepted that Gardner was a Royal Arch Freemason, as his diary suggests, then he would have accepted Gardner as the equivalent level of Royal Arch into the O.T.O. We know Gardner was a Master Mason, which is 3rd degree, and the Royal Arch is a side degree in Masonry, seen by some as being 4th degree in Freemasonry. Hence, Crowley giving Gardner a 4th degree Charter in the O.T.O. is not fast-tracking him but acknowledging the degrees Gardner had told him he had already achieved in Freemasonry.

Another line of investigation to take is to compare Gardner's Wiccan Book of Shadows to ritual material of Royal Arch Chapter Freemasonry in the same way I have compared it to Craft Freemasonry ritual material (see later). This I have done and there are couple of areas of overlap between Royal Arch ritual and Wiccan

---

Orpheus, Pentacle magazine, Autumn 2009, page 14.
56 The Triumph of the Moon: A History of Modern Pagan Witchcraft by Ronald Hutton, Oxford University Press, 1999, page 219,
57 Gerald Gardner & the Ordo Templi Orientis, by Rodney Orpheus, Pentacle magazine, Autumn 2009, page 15.
58 Modern Wicca: A History From Gerald Gardner to the Present, Michael Howard, Llewellyn, 2010, p77.

Books of Shadows. One is the use made of the Elements (see later) and the other is the concept of the veil to hide the mysteries. In Wicca there is 'The Charge: Lift Up the Veil' which we read earlier. The Veil and its use to hide the mysteries about the Tabernacle occurs in Royal Arch degree. The candidate in the Royal Arch Passing the Veil ceremony goes through a series of coloured veils: blue veil, then purple veil, then the scarlet veil and has to provide password and sign to pass each, reaching ultimately the white veil. This was the approach to the Holy of Holies of the Tabernacle and the Ark of Covenant. [59] For example in current practice:

'The Chapter would have been set up as today except that the pedestal and all that surrounds it, including the banners, would have been close to the Principals to enable them to be hidden from the candidate's sight by the white veil. The rest of the room would be divided into three by the Scarlet, Purple and Blue Veils, leaving a space between the latter and the door to the Chapter Room'. [60]

The Book of the Law by Aleister Crowley, specifically the section in the ceremony of the Opening of the Veil in the Gnostic Mass, also influenced the Wiccan Book of Shadows. The veil to the sacred mysteries is the common ground here, but in itself is not enough to shed more light on Gardner's claim to the Royal Arch degree.

Michael Howard, in *Modern Wicca: A History From Gerald Gardner to the Present,* quoting the archives of the Grand Lodge at Freemasons' Hall in London, states that *'Gardner was initiated into the first degree of*

59 Revd Neville Barker Cryer, What Do You Know about Royal Arch?, Lewis Masonic, 2002.p21.
60 For image see www.royalarchsurrey.org.uk/news_73.html

Freemasonry as an Entered Apprentice in the Sphinx Lodge in Colombo on May 23, 1910. He was then raised to the second degree on June 20, 1910, and became a Master Mason a week later on June 27. According to the Lodge's records, he resigned shortly afterwards. When Gardner met Aleister Crowley in 1947, he told him that he held the high degree of Royal Arch Mason. It is possible that he was also a Co-Mason (Co-Mason Lodges have both men and women members, such as The International Order of Freemasonry for Men and Women, Le Droit Humain), and the Bracelin biography says he 'had a soft spot for the Masonic Craft, and nowadays feels that there are close similarities in the craft of the witches; in fact he goes so far as to say that witchcraft is the original lodge'.[61]

I have contacted the Sphinx Lodge which is still operating; Gardner did not reach the office of Worshipful Master in his mother lodge, as he is not listed as one of the Sphinx Lodge's Past Masters.[62] Gardner, later in life, became a member of Crotona Fellowship which was based on Co-Masonry and was a Rosicrucian society. It was via this group that Gardner made his links with the New Forest coven, and this set him on his way to founding Wicca.

The heroine of Gardnerian Wicca was Doreen Valiente (1922-1999). I had the privilege of hearing one her last public lectures on Wicca before she passed to the Summerlands; she was insightful, knowledgeable and down to earth all at the same time. She re-wrote much of the Wiccan Book of Shadows, making it more

---

61 Modern Wicca: A History From Gerald Gardner to the Present, Llewellyn, Michael Howard, 2010, pp12-13.
62 Sphinx Lodge Past Master: www.sphinxlodge.org/past_masters.htm

accessible to a new generation.

Notably she had access to a set of notebooks which belonged to a member of the Alpha-Omega Lodge of the Golden Dawn, dated 1902-1908. These notebooks contained Golden Dawn initiation rituals for the different grades and teaching materials; she incorporated these into her personal Wiccan Book of Shadows.[63] Her access to the Golden Dawn Flying Rolls number 5 *Thoughts on the Imagination* by Dr Edmond Berridge and her work shows her interest was deep-rooted. [64] She also knew Israel Regardie, who was working and publishing relating to the Golden Dawn current, as well as being a member of Robert Cochrane's Tubal Cain's coven.

Her work with Golden Dawn material means she was also influenced by the Freemasonry current even before she started working with Gerald Gardner.[65] She was probably the first person who recognised Gerald Gardner's borrowing from other traditions and labelling the end product as an ancient continuous tradition. Indeed in her recent biography we read of: *'...the challenge to Gardner by Doreen and Ned Grove over their high priest's blatant plagiarism of the O.T.O., Golden Dawn, and other materials in the Gardner Book of Shadows. It was a wise move, as the material was bound to have been unmasked if not by them, then by subsequent researchers in the future, and would certainly have led to Wicca being totally undermined as a credible spiritual path. This effectively established Doreen as the second branch of Wicca should Gardner's*

---

63 Modern Wicca: A History From Gerald Gardner to the Present, Michael Howard, Llewellyn, 2010, p111.
64 Ameth: The Life and Times of Doreen Valiente by Jonathan Tapsell Avalonia, 2014, p18.
65 ibid.

work ultimately become discredited'.[66]

The other player in popularising Wicca was Alex Sanders, who claimed a family tradition from his grandmother and was initiated in his kitchen. He went on to form another branch of Wicca, the Alexandrian Tradition. Some online resources do suggest a link between Alex Sanders and Freemasonry; however no formal reference can be located to date. It is therefore assumed here that this link is mere speculation. Alexandrian Wicca is heavily based on Gardnerian Wicca, as a result any Masonic influences in the material come via Gardner and Crowley. While Sanders was not a Freemason, he is said to have been involved with a number of quasi-Masonic groups, the Knights Templars, the Order of Saint Michael, the Order of Saint George and the Ordine Della Luna[67], and he might have drawn from such places for ideas, meaning that the Masonic influence on Wicca was maintained up to 1970s.

Now a word on tradition; a number of times I have seen people on e-lists state that their mystery tradition goes back all the way to the Bronze age; needless to say they get a very unpleasant hammering from lots of other people on the list, and end up hanging from a metaphorical cross. Traditions rely on their stated connection to the past to justify their approach; however, this is an illusion, as each rite creates something new. It is the techniques used in rites that are old in mystery, not the schools themselves. Mystery schools in operation today should not need to overtly justify the history and age of their schools. Certain myths and techniques they, and many other groups

---

66 ibid, p89.
67 http://en.wikipedia.org/wiki/Alex_Sanders_(Wiccan)

use, work, as they have since the early days of Mankind.

The oldest continuous traditions and mystery schools in the UK are perhaps Freemasonry and Druidry. Druidry (see Appendix I), is no older than 250 years, while Freemasonry can only be traced clearly to 1717, and less clearly to the 14th century, or, perhaps back into the medieval period when there were operative masons in Europe working as Guilds.

THE ELEMENTS

Another common ground between Freemasonry and Wicca is the importance of the four elements. One of the fundamental characteristics of Wicca is the use of the four elements of Air, Fire, Water and Earth in its rituals, Spirit being seen in Wicca as the fifth element. The four elements are associated with the four cardinal directions and four points of a pentagram; the fifth, upward, point is Spirit or ether which is above the four. The four elements are used to define the sacred space with one element called upon per direction as Watchtowers or Guardians: air in the east, fire in the south, water in the west and earth in the north.

The four triangular-based symbols of the elements are used in many Wiccan and Pagan books, being inherited from the Golden Dawn system and Western alchemy. The four elemental triangles are at least old as the 1600s, and the Golden Dawn Master Masons may in turn have adapted them from medieval sources.

Air,   Fire,   Water,   Earth.

In Royal Arch Freemasonry, the elements are

incorporated into its practices in the form of the five Platonic bodies or solids. The five solids represent the four elements of this world as discussed in Plato's Timaeus. These shapes are examples of polyhedra which means 'many sides'. These are in order:

- Fire (Tetrahedron: four triangular sides)
- Air (Octahedron: eight faces)
- Earth (Hexahedron: six faces)
- Water (Icosahedron: twenty faces)
- and Universe (Dodecahedron: twelve faces).

Plato (427-347BC) associated the Tetrahedron form to the element of fire *'because of the penetrating acuteness of its edges and vertices, and because it's the simplest and most fundamental of regular solids. The Greeks also knew the tetrahedron as* puramis, *whence the word pyramid.'*[68] He assigned the Octahedron to the element of air, which is between fire and water. Furthermore *'the tetrahedron, octahedron and icosahedron are made of identical triangles, the icosahedrons are the largest. This led Plato to associate the icosahedron with water, the densest and least penetrating of the three fluid elements Fire, Air and Water'.*[69] Plato assigned the element of Earth to the hexahedron or the cube, due to the stability of its bases. The fifth element is Universe and is represented by Dodecahedron.

The Platonic bodies are part of the syllabus of teaching of the Quadrivium. The Quadrivium was thought of by Pythagoras as the Tetraktys around 500BC, whose seven subjects became known as the

---

68 Quadrivium: Number Geometry Music Heaven, Miranda Lundy, Daud Sutton, Anthony Ashton, Jason Martineau, John Martineau, Wooden Books, (2010), p134.
69 ibid, p138.

seven liberal arts and sciences. These are: Grammar, Rhetoric, Logic, Arithmetic, Geometry, Music, and Astronomy. [70] These teachings are part of modern Freemasonry and every initiate is expected to make a serious study of them. In the second degree, the initiate, after receiving their Fellowcraft apron, is told:

'Now you wear that apron, you are recognised as a Fellow of our Craft. As such, the liberal arts and sciences should be the focus of your study. Such education will help you better discharge your duty as a Mason and make you better enabled to move towards an understanding of the wonderful works of the Most High.' [71]

The importance of the Seven Liberal Arts and Sciences of Grammar, Rhetoric, Logic, Arithmetic, Geometry, Music, and Astronomy, in Freemasonry are described as:

'Grammar is the science which teaches us to express our ideas in appropriate words, which we may afterward beautify and adorn by means of Rhetoric; while Logic instructs us how to think and reason with propriety, and to make language subordinate to thought. Arithmetic, which is the science of computing by numbers, is absolutely essential, not only to a thorough knowledge of all mathematical science but also to a proper pursuit of our daily avocations. Geometry, or the application of Arithmetic to sensible quantities, is of all sciences the most important since it is through it that we are enabled to measure and survey the globe that we inhabit. Its principles extend to other spheres; and, occupied in the contemplation and measurement of the sun, the moon, and heavenly bodies, constitute the science of Astronomy. Lastly, when our minds are filled, and our

---

70 ibid, p3.
71 Turning the Hiram Key: Making Darkness Visible, by Robert Lomas, 2007, p108.

thoughts enlarged, by the contemplation of all the wonders which these sciences open to our view, Music comes forward, to soften our hearts and cultivate our affections by its soothing influences.[72]

The Seven Liberal Arts and Sciences are described in the Masonic Cooke poem dated c1420 as:

*'How and in what manner that this worthy
science of geometry began, I
will tell you, as I said before. Ye shall understand
that there be 7 liberal sciences,
by the which 7 all sciences
and crafts, in the world, were
first found, and in espwciall,
for he is causer of all, that is to
say the science of geometry of all
other that be, the which 7 sciences are called thus.
As for the first, that is called [the] fundament
of science, his name is grammar,
he teacheth a man rightfully to
speak and to write truly. The
second is rhetoric, and he teacheth a man to speak
formably and fair. The third is
dialecticus, and that science teacheth
a man to discern the truth
from the false, and commonly it is
called art or sophistry. The fourth
is called arithmetic, the which
teacheth a man the craft of
numbers, for to reckon and
to make account of all things.
The fifth [is] geometry, the which
teacheth a man all the metcon,
and measures, and ponderacion,*

---

72 The General Ahiman Rezon And Freemason's Guide by Daniel Sickels, 1868. www.sacred-texts.com/mas/gar/gar45.htm

of weights of all mans craft.
The 6th is music, that teacheth
a man the craft of song, in
notes of voice and organ,
and trumpet, and harp, and of all
others pertaining to them. The
7th is astronomy, that teacheth
man the course of the sun,
and of the moon, and of other
stars and planets of heaven.'[73]

A more modern translation by Bro. George William Speth (1847-1901) is:

These seven sciences are as follows:

The first, which is called the foundation of all science, is grammar, which teacheth to write and speak correctly.
The second is rhetoric, which teaches us to speak elegantly.
The third is dialectic, which teaches us to discern the true from the false, and it is usually called art or sophistry (logic).
The fourth is arithmetic, which instructs us in the science of numbers, to reckon, and to make accounts.
The fifth is Geometry, which teaches us all about mensuration, measures and weights, of all kinds of handicrafts.
The sixth is music, and that teaches the art of singing by notation for the voice, on the organ, trumpet, and harp, and of all things pertaining thereto.
The seventh is astronomy, which teaches us the course of the sun and of the moon and of the other stars and planets of heaven.[74]

---

73 http://freemasonry.bcy.ca/texts/cooke.html
74 http://freemasonry.bcy.ca/aqc/cooke.html

FREEMASONRY IN WICCA

'I ask you as a stranger—going to the West," he said,
with emphasis. "Where have you come from?" said I.
"From the East," said he, "and I am hoping that you will
give him the message on the Square—for the sake of my
Mother as well as your own." Englishmen are not
usually softened by appeals to the memory of their
mothers; but for certain reasons, which will be fully
apparent, I saw fit to agree.'

   - *The Man Who Would Be King,* by Rudyard Kipling.

    The influence of Freemasonry on Wicca is twofold,
firstly the direct influences, which are examined in this
chapter, and secondly the indirect influences. The
direct influences explored below are actual words,
steps, and ritual structures. The mental craft seen in
Freemasonry applies to Gardnerian Wicca and some
other Neo-Pagan branches. In Wicca, the Charges are
mostly memorised and much of the ritual texts are
recited word-perfect from memory. This feature of
Wicca is probably also inherited from Freemasonry and
is also in line with some classical pagan schools.

    Other branches of Neo-Paganism may memorise or
read from printed scripts, or use wordcraft to create
poetry, new invocations, or other original material
especially for each occasion, or spontaneously
extemporise during rites. This is a major difference to
Freemasonry, where no freeform is allowed and no new
material is included in the ceremony.

    The difference between mental craft and word craft
seen as spiritual techniques is interesting. Celtic Bards
and Druids, Indian Brahmin priests, Persian

Zoroastrian priests, and many mystery schools' religions, all required their initiates to become adept in mental craft as well as word craft and the holy texts had to be fully memorised as part of the training, In Islam, one who has memorised the entire Koran is called Hafiz. These were oral traditions which used mental craft to convey the teachings. These we can see today in Freemasonry and Gardnerian Wicca.

THE CRAFT

Freemasonry and Wicca are both known as 'the Craft'. The name of a 'thing' defines it; it is a basic part of the human language to give things which are linked a similar name.

THE WORKING TOOLS

In Freemasonry the term "Working Tools" is used. These, for the first degree are the 24-inch rule, the common lump-hammer, and the stonecutters blade (chisel)[75]. Wicca also uses the term "Working Tools", which are presented to the first-degree initiate in this order: first the Magic Sword, the Athame (black-handled knife), the white-handled knife, the Wand, the Cup, the Pentacle, the incense censer, the scourge, and lastly the cords[76].

Other magical tools and items are sometimes included by Magicians and other Neo-Pagans in their workings and on their altars (Figure: 10).

In Freemasonry, the initiate is presented with the

---

75 Turning the Hiram Key: Making Darkness Visible, by Robert Lomas, Lewis Masonic, 2007, p71.
76 The Witches Way, Janet and Stewart Farrar, Hale, 1984, p20.

working tools[77], in Wicca, at a similar point in the rite of the first-degree initiation the working tools are presented and explained to the initiate: 'Now I present to thee the Working Tools...'[78]. While the tools are different, the opening words and timing are identical. Professor Ronald Hutton also discusses the Masonic working tools in his book *The Triumph of the Moon: A History of Modern Pagan Witchcraft*, where Masonry is seen as helping to provide the structure of Wicca.[79]

Figure 10: Some example of Wiccan or Pagan Working Tools: the Sword, Wand, Chalice, Pentacle, Bell, Incense/joss stick, Candles (Photo: by Payam Nabarz).

However, on meaning and application there are differences between the traditions as seen in the table following:

---

77 Turning the Hiram Key: Making Darkness Visible, by Robert Lomas, 2007, p70.
78 The Gardnerian Book of Shadows, by Gerald Gardner, at sacred-texts.com
79 The Triumph of the Moon: A History of Modern Pagan Witchcraft by Ronald Hutton, Oxford University Press, 1999, p56-57.

Working Tool	Application	Symbolic meaning
24-inch gauge	For measurement	24 hours, to be spent in part in prayer, part in work and part in helping others
Common lump-hammer	Knock off rough lumps of stone	Our conscience to hold back negative traits
Chisel	Make the stone smooth	Education to enable one to become a more useful member of society
Square	Measure right angles in building	Differentiate between right and wrong
Level	Verify the horizontal	Equality between people
Plumb rule	Align uprights	Justice and upright actions
Centre marker	Line fixed to centre to draw out perimeter of foundation of buildings	Divine laws at the centre of our being
Pencil	Draw plans of the building	All life actions have consequences and recorded in cosmos
Compasses	Allows exact measurements	Show limits of good and evil and our place within the cosmos

Table 2: Freemason working tools compared to magical tools in Wicca. Freemason Working tools numbered 1-3 belong to the first degree, 4-6 to the second degree, 7-9 to the third degree.[80]

---

80 Based on Turning the Hiram Key: Making Darkness

The purely Wiccan Working Tools are given to the initiate as part of their first-degree rite. In Gardnerian Wicca this is described in the 1949 version as:

"Now I present to thee the Working Tools of a Witch. First the Magic Sword. With this, as with the Athame, thou canst form all Magic Circles, dominate, subdue, and punish all rebellious Spirits and Demons, and even persuade the Angels and Geniuses. With this in your hand you are the ruler of the Circle. [Here "kiss" means that the initiate kisses the tool, and the Magus then kisses the Witch being initiated.]

"Next I present the Athame. This is the true Witch's weapon and has all the powers of the Magic Sword [kiss].

"Next I present the White-Handled Knife. Its use is to form all instruments used in the Art. It can only be properly used within a Magic Circle [Kiss].

"Next I present the Wand. Its use is to call up and control certain Angels and geniuses, to whom it would not be mete to use the Magic Sword [Kiss].

"Next I present the Pentacles. These are for the purpose of calling up appropriate Spirits [Kiss].

"Next I present the Censer of Incense. This is used to encourage and welcome Good Spirits and to banish Evil Spirits. [kiss]

"Next I present the Scourge. This is a sign of power and domination. It is also to cause suffering and purification, for it is written, to learn you must suffer and be purified. Art willing to suffer to learn?"

Witch: "I am."[Kiss]

Magus: "Next, and lastly I present the Cords. They are of use to bind the sigils in the Art, the material basis, and to enforce thy will. Also they are necessary in the oath. I Salute thee in the name of Aradia and Cernunnos, Newly made Priestess and Witch." Magus strikes seven

---

Visible, by Robert Lomas, 2007. And Emulation Lodge of Improvement, Emulation Ritual, Lewis Masonic, 2007.

knells on the bell and kisses Witch again, then circumambulates with her, proclaiming to the four quarters, "Hear, ye Mighty Ones, (name) hath been consecrated Priestess and Witch of the Gods."[81]

Wiccan, Neo-Pagan and Magician's Working Tools	Application	Symbolic Meaning
Athame (black-handled blade) and/or sword	Commanding of spirits and casting magic circles.	In Gardnerian Wicca this is the tool of the element of fire and in Golden Dawn the element of air. In the Wiccan rite of Cakes and Wine represents the God (and phallus); is dipped in the chalice to symbolise divine sexual union of male and female.
White-handled blade	Some use the white-handled blade (Boline) for cutting, keeping the black-handled blade for non-physical use and purposes.	A practical knife
Cup or Chalice	To drink water or wine from	Element of Water. Represents the Goddess (and Yoni) in the symbolic Great Rite.

---

81 The Gardnerian Book of Shadows, by Gerald Gardner, at www.sacred-texts.com

Wand	To cast magic circle and direct intention and Will.	In Gardnerian Wicca, the element of Air, in some traditions seen as Fire. Represents the God in the symbolic Great Rite
The Pentacle	Talisman. Calling up appropriate Spirits To eat cake from.	Disc or Pentacle representing the Element of Earth
Book	Ritual text to read from, the Book of Shadows, or Grimoire	Knowledge
Candle	Light	Element of Fire
Incense and Censer	Invokes sense of smell, rises to heavens and welcome Good Spirits and to banish Evil Spirits	Element of Air or Spirit
Scourge	Purification, sign of power	Challenges in the path
Cords	Worn around the waist	The initiate's measure, setting of circle boundaries
Bell	Sound, music, summoning of spirit	Sound focuses the intent

Table 3: Wiccan Working Tools and other common magical tools used by Pagans and Magicians[82]

---

82 Jordan, Michael, Witches-an encyclopaedia of paganism and magic, Kyle Cathie Ltd, 1996.
The Gardnerian Book of Shadows, by Gerald Gardner, at sacred-texts.com
Rankine, David; d'Este, Sorita, Practical Elemental Magick, Avalonia, 2008.
Crowley, Aleister, Magick in Theory and Practice, Red

Table 3 describes both the Wiccan Working tools and common magical tools also used by non-Wiccans and magicians.

The Freemasons' Working Tools allow the transformation of the raw initiate or rough ashlar stone into a perfect cube, somewhat similar to the process of metamorphosis of changing grapes into wine in Sufism, or the transformation of barley to beer in the British folk song John Barleycorn.

The perfect stone then has a place in the Great Architect's mansion, the cosmic plan or, as Rudyard Kipling describes it in his poem of 1902, as a Palace:

THE PALACE

by Rudyard Kipling

When I was a King and a Mason,
a Master proven and skilled,
I cleared me ground for a Palace such
as a King should build.
I decreed and dug down to my levels.
Presently, under the silt,
I came on the wreck of a Palace
such as a King had built.

There was no worth in the fashion,
there was no wit in the plan,
Hither and thither, aimless,
the ruined footings ran,
Masonry, brute, mishandled,
but carven on every stone:
"After me cometh a Builder.
Tell him, I too have known."

Swift to my use in my trenches,

Wheel/Weiser, 1994.

where my well-planned ground-works grew,
I tumbled his quoins and his ashlars,
and cut and reset them anew.
Lime I milled of his marbles;
burned it, slacked it, and spread;
Taking and leaving at pleasure
the gifts of the humble dead.

Yet I despised not nor gloried; yet,
as we wrenched them apart,
I read in the razed foundations
the heart of that builder's heart.
As he had risen and pleaded,
so did I understand
The form of the dream he had followed
in the face of the thing he had planned.

When I was a King and a Mason,
in the open noon of my pride,
They sent me a Word from the Darkness.
They whispered and called me aside.
They said, "The end is forbidden.
" They said, "Thy use is fulfilled.
"Thy Palace shall stand as that other's,
the spoil of a King who shall build."

I called my men from my trenches,
my quarries, my wharves, and my sheers.
All I had wrought I abandoned
to the faith of the faithless years.
Only I cut on the timber,
only I carved on the stone:
"After me cometh a Builder.
Tell him, I too have known!"

THE CHARGE

There are a number of powerful and moving catechisms and teaching statements in Freemasonry that are delivered at different stages of initiation. Freemasonry refers to these statements as 'Charges'. These Charges are tools for conveying complex myths and stories. The oldest of these Charges is the Regius Poem or the Halliwell Manuscript, circa 1390. [83] There are also a number of Walking Charges, which are delivered from different parts of the lodge while walking, and which in a formal ritual format explain the history of the Craft and the morality associated with the Masonry. [84]

In Wicca there is also a 'Charge', the 'Charge of the Goddess' which is used with a similar intent to convey a deep message. It is to be read while the initiate stands, properly prepared, before the Circle and also recited as part of the Wiccan Drawing Down The Moon. While Freemasons square the circle, Wiccans meet in a circle.

Perhaps the real spirit of Wicca is not in the details of its history, but best captured in the concluding lines of the 'Charge of the Goddess' or 'The Charge: Lift Up the Veil' which we read earlier. It worth noting that the term Veil and its use to hide mysteries about the Tabernacle also occurs in Freemasonry (Royal Arch).

THE FIVE POINTS OF FELLOWSHIP

In Freemasonry, the body of Master Hiram in the third degree is lifted using the posture called the Five Points of Companionship [85] and, in the third-degree initiation, Freemason initiates state: 'I will defend the Five Points of Fellowship, in enactment as well as concept...' [86]

---

83 www.freemasons-freemasonry.com/regius.html
84 Cornelius Sinclair, The Walking Charge and other Masonic Performance Pieces, Seven Liberal Arts Press, 2014.
85 Turning the Hiram Key: Making Darkness Visible, by Robert Lomas, 2007, p177.
86 Turning the Hiram Key: Making Darkness Visible, by

This is echoed in the Wiccan third degree with a variation:

'Make open the path of intelligence between us. For these truly are the five points of fellowship (the point-up triangle above the pentacle, the symbol for the third degree), feet to feet, knee to knee, groin to groin, breast to breast, arms around back, lips to lips, by the Great and Holy Names....'[87]

In Wicca there is also a fivefold salute or fivefold kiss, which is based on this similar schema:

'Blessed be thy feet, that have brought thee in these ways;
Blessed be thy knees, that shall kneel at the sacred altar;
Blessed be thy womb, without which we would not be;
Blessed be thy breasts, formed in beauty and in strength;
Blessed be thy lips, that shall speak the sacred names.'[88]

This is one of the reasons the pentagram is a significant symbol in both Wicca and Freemasonry: it relates both to the five points of fellowship and the four elements (earth, air, fire, water) in balance under Spirit the fifth element or the upper point of the pentagram.

The Apprentice Freemason wears his white leather apron with the flap pointed upward so as to 'display all five points of the apron';[89] when a Freemason reaches the third degree he learns more about the meaning of the pentagram: *'The four points of the crossed bones*

Robert Lomas, 2007, p143.
87 The Gardnerian Book of Shadows, by Gerald Gardner, at sacred-texts.com
88 ibid, at sacred-texts.com
89 Turning the Hiram Key: Making Darkness Visible, by Robert Lomas, 2007, p78.

meeting in the skull at the centre symbolise the Five Points of Fellowship which bring us to the centre. Yet this solemn symbol of mortality contains within it five points of hope, when illuminated by the light of the bright Morning Star rising in the east.' [90]

SO MOTE IT BE

After the recitation of Prayers and Charges in Lodges, all endorse this by saying 'so mote it be'[91]. In Wiccan groups also, after prayers, invocation and charges, the initiates say 'so mote it be'. This not a simple case of saying 'Amen', but a specific act rooted in Freemasonry. It is from Freemasonry that Wicca has inherited the phrase 'so mote it be'. Professor Ronald Hutton placed the use of this phrase as a standard cry of endorsement for the late medieval (1390 AD) Charge the Regius Poem. [92] The exact phrase in the Regius Poem is[93]:

Amen! Amen! So mote it be!
So say we all for charity.

So mote it be also occurs in Crowley's Gnostic Mass which was a huge influence on Wiccan texts.

MERRY MEET, MERRY PART, MERRY MEET AGAIN

One of the most popular Wiccan phrases is 'Merry

---

90 Turning the Hiram Key: Making Darkness Visible, by Robert Lomas, 2007, p171.
91 ibid, p47.
92 The Triumph of the Moon: A History of Modern Pagan Witchcraft by Ronald Hutton, Oxford University Press, 1999, page 55.
93 http://scottishrite.org/scottish-rite-myths-and-facts/qa-so-mote-it-be/

Meet, Merry Part, Merry Meet Again' which is said at the end of rites. This too has its origins in Freemasonry, where at the end of second degree closing its stated: *'Happy have we met, Happy may we part, and happy meet again'*[94] . In *'Wicca Magickal Beginnings'* we read:

'Recording the witch trials in his book Saducismus Triumphatus (1681), Joseph Glanvill recorded the 1664 confession of the witch Elizabeth Styles, who said when they parted from their meetings the witches said "A boy! Merry Meet, Merry part" which may be the origin of the Merry meet, Merry Part, Merry Meet Again at the end of ceremonies. However, the words spoken at the end of the old second-degree Masonic initiation could also be the root of this phrase, being "Happy have we met, happy have we been, happy may we part, and happy meet again" '.[95]

This suggests that Gardner picked the 'merry meet' phrase from either the New Forest coven, which may have had links to an older coven; or that he picked it up from his Freemason days. Freemasons, in turn, had picked it up from a common source that fed both the 1664 coven and Freemasonry, the common source perhaps being that it was simply a popular phrase in that historical period.

THE CHALLENGE

In Freemasonry, during the first-degree initiation (Entered Apprentice), a dagger is placed to the chest of the initiate as he enters the Lodge. Lomas describes

---

94 Emulation Lodge of Improvement, Emulation Ritual, Lewis Masonic, 2007, p61.
95 Wicca Magickal Beginnings, Rankine, David; d'Este, Sorita, Avalonia, 2008, p107.

this as:

'...dagger was presented to your naked breast, to symbolise that, had you recklessly sought to force yourself forward, you would have been the agent of your own demise by implement; not so, however, the Brother who held it....' [96]

In Wicca at a similar timing during the ceremony and in a similar manner the initiator:

'Places the point of the sword to the Postulant's breast, he says, "O thou who standeth on the threshold between the pleasant world of men and the domains of the Dread Lords of the Outer Spaces, hast thou the courage to make the Assay? For I tell thee verily, it were better to rush on my weapon and perish miserably than to make the attempt with fear in thy heart."[97]

Interestingly, a much older example of placing a sword on the chest of the initiates can also be observed in the Roman Mysteries of Mithras. This is shown in the trials of initiations as depicted on the walls of the Capua Vetere Mithraeum, 2nd AD. There are a number of similarities between the Roman Mysteries of Mithras and Freemasonry.

PROPERLY PREPARED

The term 'properly prepared' is used both in Freemasonry and Wicca, though there are some differences between the states of preparedness.

In Freemasonry the initiate can be seen [98] as

---

96 Turning the Hiram Key: Making Darkness Visible, by Robert Lomas, 2007, p62.
97 The Gardnerian Book of Shadows, by Gerald Gardner, at sacred-texts.com
98 Lomas, Robert, The Secret Science of Masonic Initiation, Lewis Masonic, 2008. See cover for image of an initiate's

blindfolded, a cable tow around his neck, fully clothed but with breast and knee exposed, [99] and he has to 'travel before them to demonstrate due cause that he is properly prepared to become a Mason'. [100]

In Wicca initiates are 'Properly Prepared' (1953) as follows:

'Naked, but sandals (not shoes) may be worn. For initiation, tie hands behind the back, pull up to small of back, and tie ends in front of throat, leaving a cable-tow to lead by, hanging down in front. (Arms thus form a triangle at back.) When initiate is kneeling at altar, the cable-tow is tied to a ring in the altar. A short cord is tied like a garter round the initiate's left leg above the knee, with ends tucked in. Another is tied round right ankle and ends tucked in so as to be out of the way while moving about. These cords are used to tie feet together while initiate is kneeling at the altar and must be long enough to do this firmly, the knees must also be firmly tied, this must be carefully done. If the aspirant complains of pain, the bonds must be loosened slightly; always remember the object is to retard the blood flow enough to induce a trance state. This involves slight discomfort, but great discomfort prevents the trance state; so it is best to spend some little time loosening and tightening the bonds until they are just right. The aspirant alone can tell you when this is so. This, of course, does not apply to the initiation, as then no trance is desired; but for the purpose of ritual it is good that the initiates be bound firmly enough to feel they are absolutely helpless but without discomfort.' [101]

---

dress.
99 Turning the Hiram Key: Making Darkness Visible, by Robert Lomas, 2007, p43.
100 ibid, p47.
101 The Gardnerian Book of Shadows, by Gerald Gardner, at sacred-texts.com

CIRCUMAMBULATION

It is also worth noting that both in Freemasonry[102] and Wicca [103] the first-degree initiate stands in the north-east during the first part of the ceremony. It is this level of detail that really highlights the influence of Freemasonry on Wicca. The North-East corner is the place of sunrise at the summer solstice, and in Freemasonry it states where the foundation stone of great buildings are placed. Hence, the initiate in the North-East corner represents that foundation stone and from this the initiate should transform themselves to a superstructure, perfect in its parts and honourable to the builder.[104]

The initiate then moves to four cardinal points or the stations of the sun. In Wicca the initiate is led around the circle and proclaimed at the four directions (N, S, E, and W). In Freemasonry, before the first-degree initiate makes his journey, he is told:

'The Brethren stationed at the various points of the compass will take note that Mr X is about to travel before them to demonstrate due cause that he is properly prepared to become a Mason'.[105]

This is repeated again:

---

102 Turning the Hiram Key: Making Darkness Visible , by Robert Lomas, Lewis Masonic, 2007, p.47.
103 The Witches Way, Janet and Stewart Farrar, Hale, 1984, p16
104 Emulation Lodge of Improvement, Emulation Ritual, Lewis Masonic, 2007,p97.
105 Turning the Hiram Key: Making Darkness Visible, by Robert Lomas, 2007, p47.

'travelled round and round the lodge room, moving from the sunrise of the Master's chair to the meridian of the Junior Warden, to the sunset of the Senior Warden before returning via the darkness of the northern horizon.' [106]

In Wicca the Initiator leads the initiate to the cardinal points in turn and says:

'Take heed, O Lords of the Watchtowers of the East, (then South, West, North) that (initiate's name), properly prepared, will be made a Priest/Priestess and a Witch.' [107]

COWAN

In both Freemasonry and Wicca, there are vows of secrecy and penalties associated with the breaking of vows. The non-initiates are called cowans in Freemasonry and Wicca [108] and secrets are protected from cowans. A similar concept is also present in other systems: for example, non-initiates are called Pashu in Tantra, or Muggles in the fictional story of Harry Potter!

The Apprentice Freemason is told during his initiation about the role of the outer guard (Tyler) of the lodge:

'he stands outside the Lodge, holding a drawn sword, to protect the Brethren from the incursions of cowans and other eavesdroppers while making sure that candidates are well prepared to become brothers among us.' [109]

---

106 ibid, p66.
107 The Gardnerian Book of Shadows, by Gerald Gardner, at sacred-texts.com
108 Encyclopedia of Wicca & Witchcraft, by Raven Grimassi, Llewellyn, 2000, p105.
109 Turning the Hiram Key: Making Darkness Visible, by Robert Lomas, 2007, p82.

The use of the term cowan in Freemasonry is very appropriate and makes sense as it refers to a dry stone waller. According to The Oxford International Dictionary of the English Language: 'Cowan - 1598 1. Sc. One who does the work of a mason, but has not been apprenticed to the trade. 2. Hence, one uninitiated in the secrets of Freemasonry 1707. 3. slang. A sneak, eavesdropper.' And according to The Oxford English Dictionary, one who builds dry stone walls (i.e., without mortar); a dry-stone-diker; applied derogatorily to one who does the work of a mason, but who has not been regularly apprenticed or bred to the trade.'[110] The use of the word cowan in Wicca is a borrowing from Freemasonry which makes little contextual sense in Wicca; it is a copying of the term without appreciating its historical meaning. However, it further demonstrates the level of influence Freemasonry had on Wicca.

OUTER GUARD

Some covens have a Waylock during their rites, a person who is armed with a sword or staff outside the circle in the woods to keep out the uninitiated or anyone who might wander into the area and interrupt the rite. The Waylock (one who locks the way) is an important role, but this is not documented in the Book of Shadows, so it's unclear what its origin could be. However, the role of Waylock is exactly same as the role of Tyler in Freemasonry; hence it is possible this was also influenced by Freemasonry. The Tyler is also armed with a sword and stationed outside the temple, to keep out intruders and the uninitiated.

---

110 www.masonicworld.com/EDUCATION/files/dec04/cowan.htm

THE THREE DEGREES

Both Wicca and Craft Freemasonry have three degrees. The Wiccan text used here is from the 1949 Wiccan Gardnerian version; this version was compiled by Aidan A. Kelly.[111] I have made a comparison to the rite of Craft Freemasonry as described in *Emulation Ritual,* by the Emulation Lodge of Improvement (Lewis Masonic, 2007) and *'Turning the Hiram Key: Making the Darkness Visible'* by Robert Lomas (Lewis Masonic, 2007 edition). The underlined Wiccan texts below show the overlaps between Freemasonry rites as described in Lomas' book, and Wiccan rites in the Gardnerian Book of Shadows' 1949 version. In addition to using the primary source of the *Emulation Ritual* text, which Gerald Gardner would have had access to, my choice of using Lomas' text is three-fold: it is an interesting book on the initiatory journey, it is a modern publication which takes into account modern development, and it is a book that appears to be approved by Freemason lodges as it is being sold at the Freemason's Hall Museum shop.

In addition to direct influences, there are also conceptual similarities between Freemasonry and Wicca; for example, in coming to terms with death. In Wicca, this is done in the second degree with the descent into the underworld. The myth of Persephone and Hades or Inanna's journeys in the underworld is acted out; hence, in Wicca the initiate experiences a ritual death; in Freemasonry, in the third-degree, the initiate likewise goes through a ritual death, though it is focused on the murder of Hiram Abiff.

---

111 The Gardnerian Book of Shadows, by Gerald Gardner, at sacred-texts.com

The ritual death is also common among many other mystery schools including the ancient Egyptians' Osiris death and resurrection myth; however we are not covering these conceptual similarities in this work but mainly focusing on the direct influences of Freemasonry on Wicca. The conceptual similarities that exist between mystery schools are techniques that have worked for 1000s of years and are not limited to any one religion, philosophy, or mystery school.

INITIATION: THE FIRST DEGREE

The first-degree symbol in Wicca is the triangle, the second an inverted pentagram, the third an upward pentagram with a triangle floating above it.

In Freemasonry, the first degree wears his apron with pointed flap set upward to show all five points of the apron.[112]

The following are the textual sections of the Wiccan first degree which appear to be influenced by Freemasonry, the underlined words being taken directly from Freemasonry's first degree:

'Magus leaves circle by the doorway, goes to Postulant, and says, "Since there is no other brother here, <u>I must be thy sponsor</u>, as well as priest. I am about to give you a warning. If you are still of the same mind, answer it with these words: 'Perfect Love and Perfect Trust.'" <u>Placing the point of the sword to the Postulant's breast</u>, he says, "O thou who standeth on the threshold between the pleasant world of men and the domains of the Dread Lords of the Outer Spaces, hast thou the courage to make the Assay? For I tell thee verily, it were better to rush on my weapon and perish miserably than to make

---

112 Turning the Hiram Key: Making Darkness Visible , by Robert Lomas, Lewis Masonic, 2007, p78.

the attempt with fear in thy heart." Postulant: *"I have* <u>*two Passwords*</u>: *Perfect Love and Perfect Trust."* Magus <u>*drops the sword point*</u>, *saying, "All who approach with perfect love and perfect trust are doubly welcome."...*
...and <u>*ties the cord around her neck, leaving the end dangling down in front as a Cable Tow. With the Cable Tow in his left hand and the sword in his right hand, the Magus leads her sunwise around the circle to the east,*</u> *where he salutes with the sword and proclaims, "Take heed, O Lords of the Watchtowers of* <u>*the East, (name), properly prepared*</u>, *will be made a Priestess and a Witch."* <u>*Magus leads her similarly to the south, west, and north, making the proclamation at each quarter.*</u> *...*
...<u>*Take measure*</u> *...* *...*<u>*Magus: "Then say after me. 'I, (name),*</u> *in the presence of the Mighty Ones*<u>*, do of my own will and accord, most solemnly swear that I will ever keep secret and never reveal the secrets of the Art, except it be to a proper person, properly prepared, within a circle such as I am now in.*</u> *All this I swear by my hopes of a future life, mindful that my measure has been taken, and may my weapons turn against me if I break this my solemn oath.'"...*
... saying, <u>*"Now I Present to thee the Working Tools*</u> *...*

(Note, if ceremony ends here, close circle with "I thank ye for attending, and I dismiss ye to your pleasant abodes. Hail and farewell." If not, go to next degree.)' [113]

INITIATION: THE SECOND DEGREE

The following are the sections of the Wiccan second degree which appear to be influenced by Freemasonry, the underlined words being taken directly from Freemasonry's second degree:

'*...Magus binds Witch as before, but does not blindfold*

---

113 The Gardnerian Book of Shadows, by Gerald Gardner, at sacred-texts.com

her (unlike first degree, and same as Freemasonry), and circumambulates with her, proclaims to the four quarters,

Magus: "Repeat thy new name after me, I, (name), swear upon my mother's womb and by mine Honor among men and among my brothers and sisters of the Art, that I will never reveal to any at all any of the secrets of the Art, except it be to a worthy person, properly prepared, in the centre of a Magic Circle, such as I am now in. This I swear by my hopes of Salvation, my past lives, and my hopes of future ones to come, and I devote myself to utter destruction if I break this my solemn oath."

...unties the <u>Cable Tow</u> from the altar...

passes once round the Circle, proclaiming at the Four Quarters...'[114]

INITIATION: THE THIRD DEGREE

The third Degree is called the Sublime Degree of a Master Mason, and in Wicca it is also called the Sublime Degree. In Freemasonry the candidate needs to be properly prepared to be raised to the sublime degree of a Master Mason. The word sublime is from the Latin *Sublimis*, meaning lofty, an allusion properly expressive of the teaching in the final symbolic ceremony.[115]

The following are the sections of the Wiccan third degree which appear to be influences from Freemasonry:

Magus: "<u>Ere we proceed with this sublime degree</u>, I must beg purification at thy hands."

'...<u>He circumambulates, proclaiming to the four quarters</u>, "Hear, ye mighty Ones, the twice consecrate and Holy

---

114 The Gardnerian Book of Shadows, by Gerald Gardner, at sacred-texts.com
115 www.masonicdictionary.com/sublime.html

(name), High Priestess and Witch Queen, <u>is properly prepared</u> and will now proceed to erect the Sacred Altar."...

... <u>sacred place was the point within the centre of the circle, as we of old times have been taught, that the point within the centre...</u>

... "Therefore, by seed and root, and stem and bud and leaf and flower and fruit do we invoke thee, O, Queen of Space, O dew of light, O continuous one of the Heavens." Let it be ever thus, that men speak not of Thee as one, but as none, and let them not speak of thee at all, since thou art continuous, for thou art <u>the point within the circle</u>, which we adore, the fount of life without which we would not be. <u>"And in this way truly are erected the Holy Twin Pillars Boaz and Joachim [kisses breasts]. In beauty and strength were they erected, to the wonder and glory of all men."</u>...

... For these truly are <u>the 5 points of fellowship</u>: feet to feet, knee to knee, groin to groin, breast to breast, arms around back, lips to lips....' [116]

The remainder of the above section of the Wiccan ritual which is not influenced from Freemasonry is taken from Aleister Crowley's work, specifically the section in the Ceremony of the Opening of the Veil in the Gnostic Mass which reads:

The Priest:

O Circle of Stars whereof our Father is but the younger brother, marvel beyond imagination, soul of infinite space, before whom Time is ashamed, the mind bewildered, and the understanding dark, not unto Thee may we attain, unless Thine image be Love. Therefore by seed and root and stem and bud and leaf and flower

---

[116] The Gardnerian Book of Shadows, by Gerald Gardner, at www.sacred-texts.com

and fruit do we invoke Thee.[117]

Furthermore in the Book of the Law (Liber AL vel Legis) line 27 reads:

'*Then the priest answered & said unto the Queen of Space, kissing her lovely brows, and the dew of her light bathing his whole body in a sweet-smelling perfume of sweat: O Nuit, continuous one of Heaven, let it be ever thus; that men speak not of Thee as One but as None; and let them speak not of thee at all, since thou art continuous!*'[118]

---

117 Liber XV The Gnostic Mass by Aleister Crowley, at www.sacred-texts.com/oto/lib15.htm
118 Book of the Law (Liber AL vel Legis) www.sacred-texts.com/oto/engccxx.htm

CONCLUSIONS

In the above examples we have covered the direct influences of Freemasonry on Wicca. However there are further additional indirect influences of Freemasonry on Wicca. One such indirect influence can be seen in how material from the quasi-Masonic organisation O.T.O. has helped the development of Wicca.

In this book a multitude of links and similarities between Freemasonry and Wicca were demonstrated in the form of ritual materials and the number of key players in Wicca and Neo-Pagan revival who were Freemasons or had close links with it.

The links between Freemasonry and the Neo-Pagan revival are not limited to Wicca only, and in the Appendixes that follow we examine the links between Freemasonry and Druidry, Freemasonry and Traditional Witchcraft, and some related materials of interest.

The perception of the general decline of interest in Freemasonry should be re-examined in this light: while Freemasonry might be on a decline in the last few decades, its various descendants are on an increase. This implies that a greater number of people may be aligned to the original ideals of Freemasonry than may at first appear, and the social and anthropological impact of this should be borne in mind.

Furthermore, the impact of social media means that many Freemasons' Lodges, Wiccans, and Neo-Pagan groups are now online, and those interested can interact more easily and internationally with each other. Their websites are publically available, and a few clicks enable connecting with individuals or groups that could have taken months or years to connect with in the analogue world. The landscape of the modern digital world is one that benefits esoteric groups both in allowing easy connections and access to knowledge and rare sources.

In the same way that there are self-initiates and solo practitioners among Wiccans and Neo-Pagans, slowly we are going to see solo practitioners of Freemasonry, people who were not initiated into a Lodge but who learnt their Craft from reading books on Freemasonry, such as Jean-Louis de Biasi's *Secrets & Practices of the Freemasons: Sacred Mysteries, Rituals & Symbols Revealed,* (Llewellyn Publications, 2011). There are already books and websites that can help solo practitioners of Freemasonry to begin their journey, and thus we will see the spread of Freemasonry in a new way.

At the heart of both Freemasonry and Wicca there is the spiritual quest and journey, likewise seen in many other mystery schools. The Freemasons begin as a rough ashlar stone and eventually transform to a perfect cube. Freemasonry's study of the seven liberal arts and sciences educates their initiates, transforming their minds to become a living Temple to the Great Architect, while the seven graces provide them the moral compass to walk through daily life.

In Wicca the message is also clear, as stated in the Charge of the Goddess:

'To thou who thinkest to seek Me, know that thy seeking and yearning shall avail thee not unless thou knowest the Mystery. If that which thou seekest thou findest not within thee, thou wilt never find it without. For behold, I

have been with thee from the beginning; and I am that which is attained at the end of desire'[119]

The same message is also given to all Freemasons in their 3rd-degree ceremony, which is to reflect on 'that most interesting of all human studies, the knowledge of yourself'[120]. Hence, we can still hear down the centuries the echoes of Plato's teachings, and the Delphic maxim at the Temple of Apollo at Delphi:

γνῶθι σεαυτόν: **Know thyself.**

---

[119] Wiccan prayer "Charge of the Goddess" in Janet Farrar and Stewart Farrar, Eight Sabbats for Witches (London: Robert Hale, 1992), 43.
[120] Turning the Hiram Key: Making Darkness Visible, by Robert Lomas, 2007, p174.

APPENDICES

APPENDIX I:
FREEMASONRY AND DRUIDRY

Another link between Freemasonry and the Neo-Pagan revival can be traced back to the early days of Freemasonry and Druidry. The first Freemason Grand Lodge was established in 1717 at a meeting in Goose and Gridiron pub in Churchyard of St Paul's cathedral in London, and in 1723 its regulations and book of Constitution were published[121]. In the UK at least, every attempt for Wicca or any other mystery school to find an older lineage or a direct lineage to ancient mystery schools or pagan ancestors has turned out to be difficult to validate.

In the case of Druidry, while there is no direct lineage to ancient Druids, there are potentially several possible attempts at Druid Revivals which make for an interesting myth-history. The first recorded attempt at a Druid revival took place in Oxford. According to Dr. Michel Raoult in the book Druid Renaissance:

'It is said that a grove of Druids known as Cor Emrys established in the city of Oxford in 1066 CE, this name means 'City of Ambrosia' and is rich in innuendo and invokes at the same time the Pleiades constellation, the earth's magnetism, the circle of the giants of Ambrius Hill - the megalithic astronomic calendar of Stonehenge - the traditions of Atlantis and Hyperborea, and characters such as those in the Round Table cycle of

---

121 Freemasonry A Celebration of the Craft, John Hamill, and Robert Gilbert, forward by HRH Duke of Kent, Angus Books, 2004, p27.

Breton novels.'[122]

No one knows how long the mythical 1066 grove operated, but there was a second Druid Grove, which was formed in 1245 in Oxford, known as the Mount Haemus Grove. Again, no one knows how long this second revival lasted, but there was a third revival at some point, as there were representatives of 'an Oxford Grove' present at the well-known meeting in the Apple Tree Tavern in Charles Street, Covent Garden, London on 22nd September 1717, where modern Druidry was born. The Apple Tree Tavern in London was also the location in 1716 and 1717 where the first Freemason meetings took place. Druids and Freemasons drinking in the same pub would have allowed the exchange of ideas in a social setting, as well as creating the potential for overlapping memberships. Perhaps this pub meeting could be described as the first pub moot! One of the four Freemason's lodges that formed the Grand Lodge on 24th June 1717 was the Lodge at the Apple-Tree Tavern (The Lodge is now called Lodge of Fortitude and Old Cumberland No. 12) [123]; The link between Oxford and Druidry is an interesting one, as Oxford's Albion Lodge Druid group was the group into which Winston Churchill was initiated into in 1908, seven years after his initiation as a Freemason in 1901 in the 'Studholme Lodge No. 1591'.[124] Other historical figures who were, or appear to have been, interested in both Freemasonry and Druidry include William

---

122 Druid Renaissance by Philip Carr-Gomm, Thorsons, 1998, p104.
123 The History of English Freemasonry, John Hamill, Lewis Masonic, 1994, p45.
124 Winston Churchill, A Famous Man and a Freemason by W.Bro. Yasha Beresiner. www.freemasons-freemasonry.com/beresiner7.html

Stukeley, John Wood the Elder, Iolo Morganwg[125] and to some extent even William Blake. The overlaps between Druidry and Freemasonry are clearly seen in the case of the English antiquarian William Stukeley (1687–1765). In 1717 *'he became a Fellow of the Royal Society and, in 1718, joined in the establishment of the Society of Antiquaries, acting for nine years as its secretary. In 1719 Stukeley took his M.D. degree, and in 1720 became a Fellow of the Royal College of Physicians, publishing in the same year his first contribution to antiquarian literature. Stukeley was one of the first learned gentlemen to be attracted to speculative Freemasonry, newly fashionable after the appointment of the first noble Grand Master. His Diary and Commonplace Book of 6 June 1721 says: I was made a Freemason at the Salutation Tav., Tavistock Street'* [126] and according to Druid legend, in 1722 became Chief of the Order of Druids, or at least the first Druid in modern times. Professor Ronald Hutton states that Stukeley *'became, in fact, the first modern person to identify himself completely with them and to take the name of Druid. In the mid-1720s he drafted a set of books to prove his case, which, had they been published, would have been astonishingly radical for their time. They preached, boldly, a Pagan religion embodied in the old monuments which were actually valid and reflected cosmic truths. He could not, however, persuade his aristocratic friends to sponsor them, and seemed to find nobody else willing to take his Druidic faith seriously. As a result, he ended up stranded in the late 1720s, sulking in a lonely part in Lincolnshire with*

---

125 Masonic Papers by Dr Andrew Prescott, Iolo Morganwg and Freemasonry. www.freemasons-freemasonry.com/prescott10.html
126 http://en.wikipedia.org/wiki/William_Stukeley

a failing medical practice. The fact that he had redesigned his back garden as a Druid temple was of only temporary comfort to him'.[127]

The fusion of Druidry (as viewed at the time) and Freemasonry is best seen in work of John Wood the Elder in the city of Bath's Circus buildings. Its beautiful architecture is a sacred geometry which embeds dimensions of Stonehenge combined with Masonic symbolism.

When the Ancient Order of Druids (AOD) was formed in 1781 as a Friendly Society it modelled itself on Freemasonry as far as its organisational structure was concerned. Their first group was called *'Lodge No.1 of the Ancient Order of Druids, and equivalent to Masons' Grand Lodge as the executive body of the order, to which new lodges had to apply for acceptance and registration, and which would make rules for all.'* [128] The Ancient Order of Druids grew in popularity and by 1831 had reached 200,000 members[129]. AOD is still active both in UK and internationally; the Past Service jewel of AOD has a square and looks similar to the Past Master jewel of Freemasonry. AOD meet in lodges and refer to each other as Brother [130]. This is significant, as it links Druidry to Freemasonry over 100 years before the arrival of the Golden Dawn or Wicca.

---

127 The First Mount Haemus Lecture The Origins of Modern Druidry, by Professor Ronald Hutton
www.druidry.org/events-projects/mount-haemus-award/first-mount-haemus-lecture
128 Hutton, Ronald, The Druids: A History, Hambledon Continuum, 2007, p141.
129 Freemasonry and Fraternal Societies, by Dr David Harrison and Fred Lomax, Lewis Masonic, 2015, p68.
130 Ancient Order of Druids www.aod-uk.org.uk/home.htm

APPENDIX II:
FREEMASONRY AND TRADITIONAL
WITCHCRAFT

Another twist in the story comes from the potential influence of Traditional Witchcraft and Hereditary practices on Wicca. For example, there are some interesting legends about the role of the Essex Cunning Man George Pickingill (1816-1909). In the book *'The Pickingill Papers: The Origins of the Gardnerian Craft'*, by W.E. Liddell and Michael Howard (Capall Bann, 1994) a number of interesting points are made. The *Pickingill Papers* are the subject of much recent academic debate in the 2014 issues of the *Cauldron* magazine[131] between Richard Ward[132], Professor Ronald Hutton[133] and Cauldron editor Michael Howard. These make the papers and discussion around it a fascinating read. The papers which Cauldron editor Michael Howard describes as 'Craft legends' from 'Elders' of the coven[134] are of interest here with their potential links to Freemasonry. The *Pickingill Papers* suggest the following:

'A small coterie of Master Masons established a lengthy and productive relationship with Pickingill from the 1850s onwards. These Freemasons entertained 'Rosicrucian' fantasies and sought personal verification that Masonic Crafters and Rosicrucian Crafters were siblings of the Old religion. Old George awed these

---

131 Last of the Essex Cunning Men, Richard Ward, the Cauldron magazine No 152, May 2014, p17-22.
132, Richard Ward, the Cauldron magazine No 154, Autumn 2014, p46.
133 Prof Ronald Hutton, the Cauldron magazine No 153, Summer 2014, p6.
134 Mike Howard, the Cauldron magazine No 152, May 2014, p22.

Masonic *'Rosicrucians' with demonstrations of his mastery over elements. He was also able to fascinate them by expounding 'the inner secrets' of Masonry. None of these learned Masons could comprehend how this non-Mason had penetrated their Craft mysteries. It was reluctantly conceded that the witch cult may have possessed some secret arcane knowledge. Occult-minded Freemasons were to question Old George very thoroughly over a period of many years.'*[135]

Furthermore it states:

'It is no exaggeration to claim that Pickingill machinations materially influenced the founding of SRA 'Societas Rosicruciana in Anglia' (in 1865) and the GD 'Golden Dawn' (in 1888). Two Master Masons who were to become members of SRA had been accepted by Old George as his pupils. I allude to Hargrave Jennings and W.J. Hughan. Both men believed that the Masonic Craft could learn much of value from the witch cult. Pickingill freely exchanged ideas and Craft rituals with these two eminent pupils.'[136]

The system and Craft that Old George (Pickingill) practised was said by Howard to be a combination of *'Danish paganism, Arabic mysticism, Christian heresy, and French witchcraft'.*[137]

In addition to Old George, there might be other influences from Traditional Witchcraft on Wicca via other cunning men. For example, a parallel exists in the form of Mason's Word and Horseman's Word. The Horseman tradition is mentioned in an exhibit item in

---

135 Pickingill Papers the Origins of the Gardnerian Craft,
W.E. Liddel and Michael Howard (Capall Bann, 1994), p. 37.
136 Pickingill Papers the Origins of the Gardnerian Craft,
W.E. Liddel and Michael Howard, p39.
137 Modern Wicca: A History From Gerald Gardner to the
Present, Michael Howard Llewellyn, 2010, p.51.

the Library and Museum of Freemasonry in London. In the recent book *Freemasonry and Fraternal Societies*, by Dr David Harrison and Fred Lomax, a short chapter is dedicated to Horseman's Word: they report that the Society of Horseman's Word had its origins in the 18th century in Scotland and was initially a friendly society and *'had an initiation ceremony, oaths and secret passwords, and appeared to have been influenced by Freemasonry and Millers' Word'*.[138] The link between the two traditions is described in one article called The Society of the Horseman's Word which says it

'...taught a fanciful history that purported to explain the origin of the Society from the earliest times, involving biblical and mythological characters, and others that are referred to in the pseudo-history of Freemasonry, and finally, as horses were replaced by tractors, some of the members of the Society, no longer operative horsemen, retained the rituals by amalgamating with Masonic Lodges'[139].

Of course there are other threads which make up Wicca: the free festival movement, the hippy era, the Green movement, environmentalism, feminism, left-wing politics, folklore studies, archaeology, anthropology, etc... If we take the actual timelines over generations into account, one could even say that Wicca is the mother of modern paganism, the Golden Dawn its grandmother, and Freemasonry its great-grandmother. These threads are the central threads that helped to create modern Paganism, today one of fastest growing religions in the UK and the US.

However, traditional witchcraft is not the subject of

---

138 Freemasonry and Fraternal Societies, by Dr David Harrison and Fred Lomax, Lewis Masonic, 2015, p114.
139 www.olddeer.org.uk/cgi-bin/delivtext?textflist=horse03.html&index=sorted

study here, and is just added as an observation. I did once attend a talk by Paddy Slade, who claims to be a hereditary witch. What I interpreted from her talk was that traditional and folk magic were essentially the magic you practice to help you survive where you live. In her case, it was a family-type cottage near a woodland, and she learned how to be in tune with that.

This is what I call 'survival magic', aka instinct, which everyone does to lesser or greater degree. There are no written sources, or pantheons, or formal teaching structures or groups. You learn it from where you live and the people around you. You learn different things to become in tune with your surroundings - it is different if you live by the sea, inland, in cities, in villages, or in forest. Survival magic is knowing your landscape so you can survive, and folklore is part of it.

One should be clear about the question of lineages. If the question is, "were there magical practitioners going back 100s of years?", then yes: people have always been aware of following their instincts. For example, laying on your hand for healing, rubbing it better, healing with herbs, calling an object by someone's name, and harming it to harm its owner, as in sympathetic magic. If the question is, "are there organised religious pagan or mystery schools and practices going back 100s of years?", then there is no evidence of these before the 1700s. Modern Paganism came out of Gardner's Wicca from 1950s, and the biggest in influence on Wicca was the Golden Dawn around 1888 onwards, and the biggest influence on the Golden Dawn was Freemasonry.

Modern Paganism, in structure, pantheon, formal teaching, and grades, has a lot in common with Golden Dawn and Freemasonry. The Golden Dawn and Freemasonry are the biggest threads; there are of course other threads in the fabric of modern paganism, but they are probably of less historical influence.

Another common ground between Freemasonry and Traditional Witchcraft is the importance of the Biblical figure of Tubal-Cain as described in Genesis 4:22. The Passage describes the lineage of skills:

"19 Lamech took unto him two wives: the name of the one was Adah, and the name of the other Zillah.
20 And Adah bore Jabal; he was the father of those who dwell in tents, and of those who have cattle.
21 And his brother's name was Jubal; he was the father of all those who handle the harp and organ.
22 And Zillah, she also bore Tubalcain, an instructor of every artificer in brass and iron; *and the sister of Tubalcain was Naamah.*
23 And Lamech said unto his wives, "Adah and Zillah, hear my voice; ye wives of Lamech, hearken unto my speech! For I have slain a man for my wounding, and a young man for my hurt.
24 If Cain shall be avenged sevenfold, truly Lamech seventy and sevenfold."
25 And Adam knew his wife again; and she bore a son and called his name Seth. "For God," said she, "hath appointed me another seed instead of Abel, whom Cain slew."
26 And to Seth also there was born a son, and he called his name Enosh. Then began men to call upon the name of the Lord."[140]

In traditional witchcraft, Tubal-Cain also has a prominent role and an entire tradition is named after him, the 'Clan of Tubal Cain' [141]. The original coven of

---

140 The source of Biblical text:
www.biblegateway.com/passage/?search=Genesis%204&version=KJ21
141 For more information see:
www.clanoftubalcain.org.uk/spear.html

this group was founded by Robert Cochrane (1931–1966) who for a time worked as a Blacksmith for London Transport; his job might have influenced his choice of coven name (Tubal Cain)[142]. The importance of Tubal Cain in magic can read in *The Pillars of Tubal Cain* by Nigel Jackson and Michael Howard, the chapters *'The Sons of the Widow'* and *'The Temple of Solomon'* being of particular interest here. Tubal Cain is somewhat similar to the Nordic deity *Wayland the Smith*, the Greek god *Hephaestus,* who was the patron god of smiths, and Vulcan, the Roman god of smithcraft and fire. This Biblical characteristic behind Tubal Cain probably was the reason Robert Cochrane chose the name, no other explanation on the choice of coven name is provided even by experts on the subject[143]. The Pillars of Tubal Cain refers to the two Antediluvian Pillars created by Jabal brother of Jubal. Together with Tubal Cain and Naameh, these four children of Lamech inscribed all the science and knowledge of their crafts onto these pillars.[144]

Tubal Cain appears in contemporary culture in the Ray Winston film Noah (2014); the story is highly dramatized and combines various Biblical tales, and while it is an entertaining film its portrayal of Tubal Cain as the 'Hollywood baddie' is inaccurate and misleading. Another popular mention is that Tubal Cain is also referred to as 'two ball and cane' , OIO. For images of this see Figure: 11 or links below[145], which

142 Ameth: The Life and Times of Doreen Valiente by Jonathan Tapsell (Avalonia, 2014), p57.
143 Genuine Witchcraft is Explained: The Secret History of the Royal Windsor Coven and the Regency by John of Monmouth (Capall Bann Publishing, 2012).
144 The Pillars of Tubal Cain by Nigel Jackson and Michael Howard, Capall Bann Publishing, 2000), p103.
145 www.thetoyeshop.com/friendly-societies/masonic-

gets conspiracy theorists linking the fictional character James Bond 007 to him! And finally another synchronicity is the letters of O.T.O. which also looks like two balls and a cane!

Figure 11 - Freemason Tubal Cain lapel pin
(Photo: by Payam Nabarz).

In folklore, iron and metals are held to repel fairies, hence some traditional witches exclude all metals from their circles on the basis they interfere with Fae energies. Indeed, some even use flint or slate blades instead of metal ones. This probably harks back to magic as practised in the Stone Age and before metals were forged. In Freemason initiations, all metals are removed from the candidate, so the candidate has no valuables. In later degrees, the figure of Tubal Cain

regalia/jewellery-giftware/cufflinks-lapel-badges-tie-tacks-stick-pins/lapel-badge-two-ball-cane.html, and
http://letchworthshop.co.uk/cat/product_details.php?p=351 and
http://letchworthshop.co.uk/cat/product_details.php?p=794

appears as the forger of metals, perhaps as a herald of the Bronze and Iron Ages. Other related tales refer to him as turning the sword into a plough, hence bringing peace and agriculture instead of war and destruction. In Cook's manuscript, which is the second oldest Masonic text dating back to the 14th century, the two pillars and Tubal Cain are referred to:

'Ye shall understand that this son Tubal Cain was [the] founder of smiths' craft, and of other crafts of metal, that is to say, of iron, of brass, of gold, and of silver, as some doctors say, and his sister Naamah was finder of weavers-craft, for before that time was no cloth woven, but they did spin yarn and knit it, and made them such clothing as they could, but as the woman Naamah found the craft of weaving, and therefore it was called women's craft and these 3 brethren, aforesaid, had knowledge that God would take vengeance for sin, either by fire, or water, and they had greater care how they might do to save the sciences that they [had] found, and they took their counsel together and, by all their witts, they said that [there] were 2 manner of stone[s] of such virtue that the one would never burn, and that stone is called marble, and that the other stone that will not sink in water and that stone is named latres, and so they devised to write all the sciences that they had found in these 2 stones, [so that] if that God would take vengeance, by fire, that the marble should not burn. And if God sent vengeance, by water, that the other should not drown, and so they prayed their elder brother Jabal that [he] would make 2 pillars of these 2 stones, that is to say of marble and of latres, and that he would write in the 2 pillars all the science[s], and crafts, that all they had found, and so he did and, therefore, we may say that he was most cunning in science, for he first began and performed the before Noah's flood.'[146]

---

146 http://freemasonry.bcy.ca/texts/cooke.html

Tubal Cain appears in traditional witchcraft for the same reasons and characteristics.

There is also an interesting poem by Master Mason Rudyard Kipling on the subject which explains it more:

JUBAL AND TUBAL CAIN

by Rudyard Kipling

Jubal sang of the wrath of God
And the curse of thistle and thorn,
But Tubal got him a pointed rod
And scrambled the earth for corn.
Old - old as that early mould,
Young as the sprouting grain
Yearly green is the strife between

Jubal and Tubal Cain!

Jubal sang of the new found sea,
And the love that its waves divide:
But Tubal hollowed a fallen tree
And passed to the farther side.
Black - black as the hurricane wrack,
Salt as the under main
Bitter and cold is the hate they hold

Jubal and Tubal Cain!

Jubal sang of the golden years,
When wars and wounds shall cease;
But Tubal fashioned the hand-flung spears
And showed his neighbours peace.
New - new as the nine-point-two,
Older than Lamech's slain
Roaring and loud is the feud avowed, 'twixt

Jubal and Tubal Cain!

Jubal sang of the cliffs that bar
And the peaks that none may crown

But Tubal clambered by jut and scar,
And there he builded a town.
High - high as the snowsheds lie,
Low as the culverts drain
Wherever they be, they can never agree

Jubal and Tubal Cain!

APPENDIX III:
THE ROYAL STARS

The importance of the Persian Royal stars in magical and esoteric systems are discussed in my book *Stellar Magic: A Practical Guide to Rites of the Moon, Planets, Stars and Constellations* (Avalonia, 2009). The four Royal stars were recognised around 3000BC and were used as a marker of the seasons, the equinoxes and the solstices.

These stars and their constellations are:

- Aldebaran, eye of the constellation Taurus,
- Regulus, in constellation Leo,
- Antares, in constellation Scorpio,
- Fomalhaut, in the stream of the Water Bearer (Aquarius) constellations.

The two red stars of Aldebaran and Antares face each other, and the two white stars of Regulus and Fomalhaut face one another. This forms a celestial alchemy of a white light/line axis and a red light/line axis crossing + each other in mid-heaven. These are four fixed signs in astrology: Taurus (spring), Leo (summer), Scorpio (autumn) and Aquarius (winter).

The four Persian Royal stars also feature in Christianity. The four faces of the Cherubim (in the Bible Book of Ezekiel. 1:10, 10:14) are the four Royal Stars. The faces of Cherubim are the lion, eagle, man, and ox. The four Royal stars (four creatures) are said to be found on each side of the throne of God (the Bible Book of Revelation 4:7). The four Royal stars and their constellations also feature in Christianity as the four Evangelists as well as the Cherubim. The symbols for the four Evangelists are:

- Matthew as Human/Angel (Aquarius),
- Mark as Lion (Leo),
- Luke as Ox (Taurus),
- John as Eagle (Aquila/Scorpio).

Figure 12 - Rosy Cross of the Hermetic Order of the Golden Dawn (Image: public domain, Wiki).

Those familiar with the Golden Dawn system and Rider-Waite tarot deck will recognise the four Cherubim on the four corners of the World and Wheel of Fortune cards in the pack. The four Cherubim were also prominently displayed on the Golden Dawn warrant of their Osiris Temple. These four constellations also feature prominently on the Rosy Cross of the Hermetic Order of the Golden Dawn (see Figure: 12)

From being worshipped on the tops of Babylonian Ziggurats, the four Royal stars found their way into ancient Greco-Roman astrology and eventually into Christianity and Kabbalah. Down the centuries they become incorporated as Watchtowers by John Dee in his Enochian magic, finally reaching modern-day magicians in the form of the four Lords of the Watchtowers in Wicca and Golden Dawn. These four stars and their constellations are a fundamental part of esoteric schools and appear in systems rooted in ancient teachings.

Therefore, it is no surprise that we find the four figures of Eagle, Lion, Man and Ox as symbols in Freemasonry. In fact, they are of such importance that these four figures appear on the shield of the United Grand Lodge of England. Furthermore, they are also present in Royal Arch Freemasonry, where the four banners of Eagle, Lion, Man and Ox are hung in the East, and are explained in the Symbolic Lecture as:

'The four principal banners represent the leading standards of the four divisions of the army of Israel, which bore devices of a Man, a Lion, an Ox and an Eagle. A Man to personify intelligence and understanding; a Lion to represent strength and power; an Ox to denote the ministration of patience and assiduity; and an Eagle to indicate the promptness and celerity with which the will and pleasure of the Great I AM are ever executed.'[147]

---

147 Domatic Chapter Of Instruction, The Ritual Of The Holy Royal Arch As Taught By The Domatic Chapter Of Instruction, No 177, Lewis Masonic, 2006, p68.

APPENDIX IV:
THE SUFI AND THEOSOPHICAL INFLUENCES ON WICCA AND PAGANISM

In addition to Freemasonry, there were also other influences in the early days of the Wicca and Neo-pagan revivals, such as the study of folklore and its incorporation into modern practices. The works of authors which inspired the Neo-Pagan revival include the groundbreaking book *The Golden Bough,* published in 1890 by Sir James Frazer (1854–1941); the works of historian Margaret Murray (1863–1963), especially her *The Witch-cult in Western Europe* (1921), and *God of the Witches* (1931); and Robert Graves' (1895–1985) *The White Goddess*, published in 1948.

In addition to the influence of the above books which looked at the ancient European ideas of paganism, other influences and threads in the creation of the Wicca and Neo-Pagan revival are from Eastern sources and traditions, which also helped to fill some of the practical technique and knowledge gaps left behind with the fall of Paganism and rise of Christianity. A brief analysis of the impact of Eastern traditions on Wicca and Neo-Paganism revival is of interest.

There has been a huge influx of Eastern religious and spiritual ideals into the West for a very long time, Christianity, Judaism and Islam being the major ones. The influence of traditional ideas in Hinduism, Tantra, and Buddhism resulted in the modern Theosophical movement which can be traced back to Helena Blavatsky (1831-1891) and her teachers. Its philosophy emphasizes a knowledge of divine things or knowledge derived from insight and experience as well as intellectual study, its name being a fusion of the Greek *Theos* (god, divinity) and *Sophia* (wisdom). The influence of Buddhism and Hinduism in the West have all been discussed at great length by many writers in the past. The influence of early 20th century Eastern mystics such as G.I. Gurdjieff is still present today. Some Pagan writers take the Eastern Sufi and Theosophical influence on western Paganism further back to Moorish and Saracen presences in Spain.

In the *Pickingill Papers,* the author goes as far as suggesting that the 'black man'[148] who appeared during witches' initiations may have been drawn from wandering Saracens helping to build a magical group! Idris Shah also made this point in the Coalmen chapter in his book, *The Sufis.* 'El-Aswad, the Black Man, is one of the important and mysterious figures in both Northern European and Spanish-Arab accounts of witchcraft rites in many parts of Europe'[149]. This kind of influence is hard to pin down, nevertheless it should be noted that in the tales of King Arthur and his Knights of the Round Table there are three Saracen knights: the three brothers Sir Safir, Sir Palomides, and Sir Segwarides. They have seats at the Round Table (Figure: 13) and play their parts in the various quests, including the Grail Quest. Sir Palomides and Sir Safir are even included in the Winchester round table which was built c.1290. The word Safir translates as Ambassador, which makes me wonder if he was originally a Saracen ambassador.

An interesting example of contacts between England and the Islamic world is seen in the gold coin of Offa, the King of Mercia in England (757- 796). The

---

148 Pickingill Papers the Origins of the Gardnerian Craft, W.E. Liddel and Michael Howard (Capall Bann, 1994), p. 136.
149 The Sufis, Idries Shah (Jonathan Cape, 1971), p179.

coin shows 'Offa Rex' on one side and an Islamic text from the Quran on the other; the coin itself is similar to an Islamic Abbasid period dinar coin. Whilst the question of how an Islamic coin came to be minted in England remains to be fully explained, there are examples of the reverse process too: early Islamic coins imitated those used in the Persian Sassanian (Zoroastrian) and Byzantine (Christian), empires. For example, some still showed the Zoroastrian fire altar on one side and the head of the Sassanian king on the other; but have Arabic text from the Quran added. The old trade routes allowed the flow of goods and all types of knowledge, and coins were the universal language spoken by all; be they Zoroastrian, Christian, Moslem or any other faith.

The exchange of knowledge and trade between the Islamic world and Western Europe could also be seen during the Viking era. *'Viking expansion from the Scandinavian homelands during their era created a cultural network with contacts from the Caspian Sea to the North Atlantic, and from the Arctic Circle to the Mediterranean'*[150]. Their expansion reached the Caspian Sea mainly via trade, but 'a raid south of the Caspian Sea into modern Iran took place in 913AD'[151] as well as invading and holding a city in modern Azerbaijan in 943AD[152], showing how far east the Vikings made it, as well as west, discovering North America before Columbus.

From trade, the gold coins from the Islamic world

---

150 Vikings life and legend exhibition British Museum in 2014.
151 Vikings: life and legend by Gareth Williams, Peter Pentz, Matthias Wemhoff, (British Museum Press, 2014), p82.
152 Vikings: life and legend by Gareth Williams, Peter Pentz, Matthias Wemhoff, (British Museum Press, 2014), p82.

made it back to Scandinavian homelands and Northern Europe. Valuables purchased from the trade route, especially gold coins from the Islamic world were of great value and prestige, so much so that some gold jewellery produced in Scandinavia imitated Islamic kufic calligraphy. A related book of interest is *Ibn Fadlans' journey to Russia: a tenth-century traveller from Baghdad to the Volga River* by Professor Richard Frye (Markus Wiener, 2006). This book is one of the sources for the fictional book *Eaters of the Dead* by Michael Crichton which was adapted into a major Hollywood film as *The 13th Warrior*.

Another stream of Sufi influence can perhaps be seen in the troubadours, whose ideals of courtly love and poetry were an echo of Sufi poetry and devotional music.

Finally, last but not least, the Knight Templars and others returning from the Crusades brought back with them Sufi and other Eastern spiritual ideas into the Western mysteries. However, what are rarely discussed are the effects and inspirations certain Sufi thoughts had at the end of the 19th century in the revival of Western esoteric orders. The modern Knight Templars are additional degrees or a side order of Freemasonry and are very active[153].

In the book *Great Satan Eblis* by Sufi Master Dr. J. Nurbakhsh, the views of many Sufi masters on Eblis (Lucifer) as a noble figure, are beautifully discussed.[154] The path Eblis has taken to reach Divine union with 'Allah' is seen by some orthodox Muslims as a left-hand

---

153 For further details on modern Knight Templars see: www.glmmm.com/kt/default.aspx
154 Great Satan Eblis by Dr.J.Nurbakhsh, Khaniqahi Nimatullahi Publications (KNP), 1986.

path. In Sufism, Eblis is not seen as God's arch-adversary: Eblis because of his love of God, would not prostrate before Adam. He is a jealous lover who would rather be punished by God than share him with those of clay. The cause of his fall is not seen as pride but jealousy.

Figure 13 - Sir Safir is seated as the 16th Knight going clockwise from King Arthur (seat 1) in the Winchester round table. King Arthur sits with a total of 24 Knights at this round table which was built c.1290. (Photo: by Payam Nabarz)

Such radical ideas were taken up by western occultists. For example, in 1910, the book *The Scented Garden of Abdullah the Satirist of Shiraz* (Persian: *Bagh-I-Muattar Haj Abdullah Shirazi*) was published. The author behind this was Aleister Crowley, who was fascinated by the Persian language, revelled in the ideas of Sufis and had travelled widely in the Middle East as well as India. Haj-Abdullah Shirazi was a character created by Crowley, after his learning of the modern Persian language, to convey his ideas based on

Sufi symbols. One modern Sufi, in an online discussion forum, described his book as 'someone splattering his ego in the garden, simply pornography, which lacked anything of any depth'. I guess being able to annoy local mystics wherever he went, by playing devil's advocate, is perhaps one of the main consistencies in Crowley's life.

The *Scented Garden of Abdullah* consists of 42 Ghazals (Persian poetic verses) and short stories, some of which refer to his male lover back in Cambridge. Even a century after their first publication, due to their highly erotic nature, orthodox Muslims can see them as obscene and blasphemous. However, Crowley was not the first Westerner who invented his own Sufi poet: Sir Francis Burton published in 1880 Sufi couplets of Haji Abdu El-Yezdi: *The Kasidah of Haji Abdu El-Yezdi: 'A Lay of Higher Order'.*

There are other Sufi influences in Crowley's work too, for example his ARARITA formula (Liber DCCCXIII vel ARARITA) begins with verses (Surah 112) from the Koran:

'Qul huwallaahu ahad
Allahus samad
Lam yalid wa lam yuulad
Wa lamyakun lahuuu kufuwan ahad'

Which Crowley describes as: *'O my God! One is Thy Beginning! One is Thy Spirit, and Thy Permutation One'.*

Crowley is best known for his books on Magick, his involvement in the fragmentation of the Hermetic Order of the Golden Dawn, and his subsequent publication of their texts, which led to an explosion of interest in mysticism. Members of the Hermetic Order of the Golden Dawn, which was founded in 1888, were already familiar with much of Eastern philosophy. The breakage of this Order occurred in 1903, and its members divided into those who wanted, for want of a better word, a left-hand path approach, and those who believed in a more puritan (right-hand path) approach. The puritan societies and ideas that resulted from this breakage have come to be known as the modern Western Mysteries. These groups subscribe to the mystery traditions of Egypt and Eleusis as well as those involving Druidic and sometimes Kabbalistic influences. These groups paved the way for the sudden rise of interest in mysticism in the Hippy era.

In Germany, the Ordo Templi Orientis (Order of the Oriental Templars) was founded in 1902 by Karl Kellner (1851-1905) who, during his extensive travels in the East, was initiated by the Arab Fakir Soliman Ben Aifha and the Indian yogis Bhima Sen Pratap and Sri Mahatma Agamya Guru Paramahamsa. The fusion of Sufism and Tantra within the O.T.O. kept on developing. Soon, after the publication of the '*Scented Garden of Abdullah*', Aleister Crowley was contacted by the O.T.O. and travelled to Germany and met Theodor Reuss [155] (1855-1923). Crowley was initiated into the O.T.O. in 1910, after which he profoundly influenced the development of the rites of the O.T.O. Crowley was running things from 1922, but it wasn't until Reuss's death in 1923 and more debate that Crowley formally became head of O.T.O in 1925. Elements of the Rites of Memphis and Misraim were also adopted by the Order.

The O.T.O. is also an offspring of Freemasonry as all its founders were Freemasons, and, in its early days, being a Freemason was a prerequisite for

---

155 For further information on Theodor Reuss see: Irregular Freemasonry in Germany, 1900-23 by Ellic Howe www.freemasonry.bcy.ca/aqc/reuss/reuss.html

entrance into its higher degrees; hence a great deal of Freemasonry's symbology and techniques etc. are found in the rites of the O.T.O. The O.T.O. being a quasi-Masonic organisation, meant that in its early days, Freemasons and Co-Masons could join the O.T.O. at the same degrees they held in Freemasonry. [156]

The Sufi connection is best seen in the third degree of the O.T.O. where, instead of commemorating the murder of Hiram Abiff, as Freemasonry does, the O.T.O. marks the murder of the Sufi master and martyr, Mansur Al Hallaj. The O.T.O. enacts the mystery around the death of Hallaj in the same way that Freemasons mark the mystery of Hiram Abiff, the Master Builder. Hallaj was martyred on March 26th 922AD for heresy as a result of making statements like *Anā l-Haqq* 'I am The Truth', and 'There is nothing wrapped in my turban but God' and 'There is nothing in my cloak but God' when he was in mystical trance. These teachings of Hallaj are present in the third degree of the O.T.O. We cannot overstate the importance of Hallaj in Sufism, and the incorporation of Hallaj into the O.T.O. is highly significant.

The left-hand path (LHP) philosophy within the O.T.O. kept on growing, and found an even wider audience when Gerald Gardner, the British founder of Wicca, was initiated into the 9th grade of the O.T.O. Gardner himself had travelled greatly in the East, and, according to 'Witches: an Encyclopaedia of Paganism and Magic' by Michael Jordan, was a Sufi initiate[157]. However, his being a Sufi initiate is not mentioned in

---

156 Gerald Gardner & the Ordo Templi Orientis, by Rodney Orpheus, Pentacle magazine, Autumn 2009, p.15.
157 'Witches-an encyclopaedia of paganism and magic' by Michael Jordan Kyle Cathie Ltd, 1996, p87.

Gardner's biography by Idris Shah. Gardner was a friend of Shah, the most prominent Sufi writer in the West, who wrote Gardner's biography 'Witch' under the alias Jack Bracelin, another mutual friend. It has been suggested that Shah didn't use his own name as he probably didn't want to be associated publicly with Wicca, whilst Jack Bracelin was already doing a great deal to catch the eye of the media. Shah's Octagon Press published Gardner's biography in 1960. Idris Shah's proposal in his classic book 'Sufis' (1964), regarding the influence of Sufism on medieval Witch cults in Europe via Spain was probably inspired by his workings with Gardner. Shah has proposed a number of potential Sufi influences on magical lore in the medieval period. To name a few: Moorish dance (or Morris dance, which is disputed), witch's athame (blood-letter), Rosicrucian ideology, the Knight Templars and Baphomet!

It is fascinating to note that several of the central figures in the revival of Neo-Paganism were linked to Sufism as well as Freemasonry. The influence of Sufism on Paganism has still continued and can be seen in the works of Andrew Chumbley and his branch of 'Sabbatical Witchcraft'. Chumbley's book 'Qutub' was published in 1995, and consists of 73 short ghazals. Qutub is a Sufi word for the magical Pole or point of spiritual orientation, and the book contains many poems and calligraphy based on Sufism. This Sufi current in Western Magic is still being manifested and most recently can seen in the publication of the 'Rumi Tarot' in 2009 by Nigel Jackson, in which he combines his beautiful artwork with Rumi's Sufi poetry.

A final note: when dealing with the history of esoteric material, proceed with caution - there are people who really think the Necronomicon is an ancient text, written by the Arab mage Abdual Alhazred! It is in fact a modern work, and like many other approaches, as mentioned before, attempts to give itself an ancient history. A question to ask for any tradition is, "does it work for you?" Rather than bothering about how old it is. The proof is in the pudding.

To bring the topic back from Eastern material and Sufism to Freemasonry, and thereby fully square the circle, it is worth noting that East-West spiritual influences are bidirectional. For example, when Freemasonry was introduced from the West to the Arab world and the Middle East in the 19th century, it was seen in some areas as a Sufi order. For example, in Turkey the word 'rite' in 'Ancient and Accepted Scottish Rite' was replaced with the word 'Tariqa' (Sufi path). This means it was seen as the *'Ancient and Accepted Scottish Sufi Path'*.[158] The way some Sufis recognised Freemasonry as another Sufi order in the 19th-century points to a number of factors including the similarity of Muslim Guilds to the original operative Stone Masons' Guilds and the universality of ritual techniques used by mystery schools and Chivalric orders. Professor Thierry Zarcone's work *Gnostic/Sufi Symbols and Ideas in Turkish and Persian Freemasonry and in Masonic-Inspired Organisations* is key reading for understanding this link.

Some of these similarities are described in *Secret Practices of the Sufi Freemasons: The Islamic Teachings at the Heart of Alchemy* by Baron Rudolf Von

---

158 Gnostic/Sufi Symbols and Ideas In Turkish & Persian Freemasonry and in Masonic-Inspired Organisations, by Professor Thierry Zarcone, the Canterbury papers vol5, Knowledge of the heart: Gnostic Movements and Secret Traditions, Lewis Masonic, 2006, p118.

Sebottendorff with introduction and translation by Stephen E. Flowers (Inner Traditions, 2013). The book states that it *'reveals the secret spiritual exercises of the Bektashi Order of Sufis as well as how this Order, also known as Oriental Freemasonry, preserves the ancient spiritual doctrines forgotten by modern Freemasonry'*. Baron Rudolf Von Sebottendorff (1875–1945) was a Freemason and involved with Sufism, and explains how in his view the mysteriously abbreviated letters found in the Qur'an represent formulas for perfecting the spirit of the individual. He also demonstrates how some of the Freemason grips are also in use by Bektashi Order of Sufis. His proposal of hand gestures and grips having meditative origins is somewhat echoed decades later by Robert Lomas in his *Turning the Hiram Key: Making Darkness Visible* [159], who also talks of how postures in Freemason initiation focus energies in the body and how Masonic postures may be acting in a similar manner to the Alexander Technique. I think both Lomas and Baron Rudolf Von Sebottendorff are onto something very significant here: if their assertions are correct then there is a great deal more to Masonic ritual than just the teaching of moral virtues. If Masonic gestures and postures are in fact akin to other practices that use bodily postures to focus the body's energies (which my own experiences of Tai Chi and Yoga also support), then Freemasonry has preserved much more ancient esoteric knowledge than at first appears. If one intones the Masonic words, these have an effect like that of Mantras, while the Masonic steps, gestures and signs could be performed in a meditative manner and with controlled breathing. Such an experimental approach could open the door to a whole

---

159 Turning the Hiram Key: Making Darkness Visible, by Robert Lomas, 2007, 205-209.

new level of understanding of the Masonic system.

Robert Graves, in his Introduction to the book *Sufis* by Idries Shah, even goes so far as to say: *'The Sufis are an ancient spiritual Freemasonry whose origins have never been traced or dated; ...the Sufi are at home in all religions: just as the Free and Accepted Masons lay before them in their lodges whatever sacred book: Bible, Koran or Torah, is accepted by the temporal State.'*[160]

As well as the common elements, there are also a number of differences between Freemasonry and Sufism. For example, while both focus on 'acts of service' to humanity and all creatures, service and charity being a cornerstone in both traditions, in Sufism the teaching is to put others first and before yourself (self-sacrifice to help others), while in Freemasonry the teaching is to help friends or others in need without detriment to oneself or one's connections. This is one of the most significant differences between the two traditions.

The development of rites by Crowley within the O.T.O. would be a major influence on the rituals of Wicca. For example, in the O.T.O's Gnostic Mass, (where the space is arranged similarly to a Freemason's Lodge), a Mass takes place, whose text is one of the sources of the Wiccan Great Rite and the Charge of the Goddess. Textual comparison shows that the Charge of the Goddess appears to be based partly on the Gnostic Mass and partly on the Book of the Law (Liber AL vel Legis) by Aleister Crowley, specifically the sections 'The Ceremony of the Opening of the Veil' in the Gnostic Mass, and line 27 of the Law of Liberty in the Book of

---

160 The Sufis, Idries Shah (Jonathan Cape, 1971), p ix.

the Law. A full textual analysis of the Charge of the Goddess can be read in Chapter 11 of *Wicca Magickal Beginnings* by Sorita d'Este and David Rankine (Avalonia, 2008) [161].

---

161 Chapter 11 of Wicca Magickal Beginnings, by Sorita d'Este and David Rankine (Avalonia, 2008) or online at http://sorita.co.uk/articles/wicca-history/charge-of-the-goddess-textual-analysis/

APPENDIX V:
THE FEAST

The sharing of food and drink after ceremonies in the form of a ritual feast are common amongst both ancient and modern pagan and other types of esoteric groups. For example, the Mithraic feast in Roman times (Figure: 14). The sacred meal was enacted by the followers of Mithras during initiation rituals, where Pater represented Mithras, Heliodromus represented the sun, and the other initiates sat around and shared the sacred meal. The feast was brought by the torchbearers of Mithras—Cautes (dawn, spring equinox) and Cautopates (dusk, autumn equinox)—to a meal where Sol and Mithras sit together.[162]

Figure 14 - Mithraic communion and ritual meal. The table is the body of the bull, two columns are also present on either side. From left, Corax- and Perses-grade initiates approach while carrying a drinking horn. On the right, a Leo and another figure (Miles-grade perhaps) approach. Pater (Mithras)

---

162 The Mysteries of Mithras: The Pagan Belief That Shaped the Christian World, by Payam Nabarz, (Inner Traditions, 2005).

*and Sol are at the table. In front is what might be a plate with
four round loaves of bread marked with a +.
(From The Mysteries of Mithra, by Franz Cumont. New York:
Dover, 1956, originally published 1903)*

The sharing of a ritual meal (Sofrh) after the
meditation and Zekr (Mantra) is also a very significant
part of some Sufi orders. The sharing of a meal is a
common ground between well-established traditions.

An important aspect of Freemasonry is also the
formal feast after the ceremony, called the Festive
Board. The Stewards of the Lodge are responsible for
serving the wine in the Festive Board, and in some
Lodges, where catering is in-house; the Stewards also
serve the food. The Officer Jewel of the Stewards is the
Cornucopia (horn of plenty) between the legs of a pair
of compasses extended. Once more Master Mason
Rudyard Kipling has expressed this aspect of Masonic
practice beautifully.

BANQUET NIGHT

*"Once in so often," King Solomon said,
Watching his quarrymen drill the stone,
"We will club our garlic and wine and bread
And banquet together beneath my throne.
And all the Brethren shall come to that mess
As Fellow Craftsmen--no more and no less.*

*"Send a swift shallop to Hiram of Tyre,
Felling and floating our beautiful trees,
Say that the brethren and I desire
Talk with our Brethren who use the seas.
And we shall be happy to meet them at mess
As Fellow Craftsmen--no more and no less.*

"Carry this message to Hiram Abif--
Excellent Master of forge and mine:
I and the Brethren would like it if
He and the Brethren will come to dine
(Garments from Bozrah or morning-dress)
As Fellow Craftsmen--no more and no less.

"God gave the Hyssop and Cedar their place--
Also the Bramble, the Fig and the Thorn--
But that is no reason to black a man's Face
Because he is not what he hasn't been born.
And, as touching the Temple, I hold and Profess
We are Fellow Craftsmen--no more no less."

So it was ordered and so it was done,
And the hewers of wood and the Masons of Mark
With foc'sle hands of the Sidon run
And Navy Lords from the Royal Ark,
Came and sat down and were merry at mess
As Fellow Craftsmen--no more and no less.

The Quarries are hotter than Hiram's forge,
No one is safe from the dog-whips' reach.
It's mostly snowing up Lebanon gorge,
And it's always blowing off Joppa beach;
But once in so often, the messenger brings
Solomon's mandate: "Forget these things!
Brother to Beggars and Fellow to Kings,
Companion of Princes-forget these things!
Fellow Craftsman, forget these things!"

BIBLIOGRAPHY

Barrett, David V, A Brief History of Secret Societies: An unbiased history of our desire for secret knowledge, Robinson, 2007.

Barrett, David V. The Atlas of Secret Societies, Octopus Publishing Group, 2008.

Bernheim, Alain, United Grand Lodge and United Grand Lodges of Germany 1946-1961, Ars Quatuor Coronatorum, Vol 127 2014.

Black, Jonathan, The Secret History of the World, Quercus, 2010.

Bogdan, Henrik, Western esotericism and rituals of initiation, State University of New York Press, 2007.

Booth, Martin, A Magick Life: a biography of Aleister Crowley, Coronet Books, 2000.

Bott, Adrian, The Great Wicca Hoax - Part I, White Dragon Magazine, Lughnasa 2001.

Bott, Adrian, The Great Wicca Hoax II: Attack of the Crones, White Dragon Magazine, Lughnasa 2002.

Buchanan-Brown, John and Chevalier, Jean and Gheerbrant, Alain, The Penguin Dictionary of Symbols, Penguin Books Ltd, 1996.

Carr-Gomm, Philip, Druid Renaissance, Thorsons, 1998.

Churton, Tobias, The Magus of Freemasonry: The Mysterious Life of Elias Ashmole - Scientist, Alchemist and Founder of the Royal Society, Inner Traditions Bear and Company, 2006.

Cotterell, Arthur, The Ultimate Encyclopaedia of Mythology, Hermes House, 2003.

Crowley, Aleister, Magick in Theory and Practice, Red Wheel/Weiser, 1994.

Crowley, Aleister, Liber XV 'The Gnostic Mass', Liber AL vel Legis, Liber DCCCXIII vel ARARITA, sacred-texts.com

Cryer, Revd Neville Barker, What Do You Know about Royal Arch?, Lewis Masonic, 2002.

de Biasi, Jean-Louis, Secrets & Practices of the Freemasons: Sacred Mysteries, Rituals & Symbols Revealed, Llewellyn Publications, 2011.

Dedopulos, Tim, The Secret World of the Freemasons, Carlton Books Ltd, 2009.

Domatic Chapter of Instruction, The Ritual Of The Holy Royal Arch As Taught By The Domatic Chapter Of Instruction, No 177, Lewis Masonic, 2006.

Emulation Lodge of Improvement, Emulation Ritual, Lewis Masonic, 2007.

Farrar, Janet and Stewart, The Witches Way, Hale, 1984.

Farrar, Janet and Stewart, Eight Sabbats for Witches, Robert Hale, 1992.

Faulks, Philippa, and Cooper, Robert L D, The Masonic Magician: The Life and Death of Count Cagliostro and His Egyptian Rite, Watkins Publishing, 2008.

Faulks, Philippa, and Skidmore, Cheryl. A Handbook for the Freemason's Wife, Lewis Masonic, 2009.

Flowers, Stephen E. introduction and translation by Baron Rudolf Von Sebottendorff, Secret Practices of the Sufi Freemasons: The Islamic Teachings at the Heart of Alchemy, Inner Traditions, 2013.

Gardner, Gerald, The Gardnerian Book of Shadows, www.sacred-texts.com/pag/gbos/index.htm

Gilbert, R. A. The Magical Mason: Forgotten Hermetic Writings of William Wynn Westcott, Physician and Magus (Roots of the Golden Dawn Series), Aquarian Press (1983).

Gilbert, RA, Revelations of the Golden Dawn The Rise and Fall of a Magical Order, W Foulsham & Co Ltd, 1997.

Hamill, John, The History of English Freemasonry, Lewis Masonic, 1994.

Hamill, John and Gilbert, Robert, forward by HRH Duke of Kent, Freemasonry A Celebration of the Craft, Angus Books, 2004.

Harrison, David and Lomax, Fred Freemasonry & Fraternal Societies, Lewis Masonic, 2015.

Heselton, Philip, Wiccan Roots, Cappall Bann, 2000.

Howard, Michael, Modern Wicca: A History From Gerald Gardner to the Present, Llewellyn, 2010.

Howard, Michael, The Cauldron magazine No 152, May 2014.

Howe, Ellic, Magicians of the Golden Dawn: A Documentary History of a Magical Order, 1887-1923, Aquarian Press, 1985.

Hutton, Ronald, The Triumph of the Moon: A History of Modern Pagan Witchcraft, Oxford University Press, 1999.

Hutton, Ronald, Witches, Druids and King Arthur, Hambledon Continuum, 2003.

Hutton, Ronald, The Druids: A History, Hambledon Continuum, 2008.

Hutton, Ronald, The First Mount Haemus Lecture The Origins of Modern Druidry, http://www.druidry.org/events-projects/mount-haemus-award/first-mount-haemus-lecture

Hutton, Ronald, Response to Pickingill article, The Cauldron magazine No 153, Summer 2014.

Hoffer, Peter, 25 years of Freemasonry in Eastern Europe, The Square magazine, December 2014.

Jackson, B. Keith, Beyond the Craft, Lewis Masonic, 2012.

Jackson, Nigel; Howard, Michael, Pillars of Tubal Cain, Capall Bann Publishing, 2000.

Jordan, Michael, Witches-an encyclopaedia of paganism and magic, Kyle Cathie Ltd, 1996.

John of Monmouth, Genuine Witchcraft is Explained: The Secret History of the Royal Windsor Coven and the Regency, Capall Bann Publishing, 2012.

Kelly, Adrian, Crafting the Art of Magic, Book I A History of Modern Witchcraft, 1939-1964, Llewellyn, 1991.

Lamond, Frederic, Fifty Years of Wicca, Green Magic, 2004.

Virtual Lodge of Instruction the producers, The Virtual Lodge of Instruction multimedia software, Lewis Masonic the suppliers, 2014.

Lomas, Robert, The Secrets of Freemasonry Revealing the Suppressed Traditions, Robinson, 2006.

Lomas, Robert, Turning the Hiram Key: Making Darkness Visible, Lewis Masonic, 2007 edition.

Lomas, Robert, The Secret Science of Masonic Initiation, Lewis Masonic, 2008.

Liddel, WE. and Howard, Michael Pickingill Papers the Origins of the Gardnerian Craft, Capall Bann, 1994.

Morgan, Pat, The Secrets of the Freemasons, Arcturus, 2006.

Nabarz, Payam, The Mysteries of Mithras: The Pagan Belief That Shaped the Christian World, Inner Traditions, 2005.

Nabarz, Payam, Stellar Magic: A Practical Guide to Rites of the Moon, Planets, Stars and Constellations, Avalonia, 2009.

Naudon, Paul, The Secret History of Freemasonry: Its Origins and Connection to the Knights Templar, Inner Traditions, 2005.

Nurbakhsh Dr.J. Great Satan Eblis, Khaniqah Nimatullahi Publications, 1986.

Orpheus, Rodney, Gerald Gardner & the Ordo Templi Orientis, Pentacle magazine, Autumn 2009.

Power, George, a Masonic miscellany, Tracingboards.com, 2004.

Rankine, David; d'Este, Sorita, Practical Planetary Magick, Avalonia, 2007

Rankine, David; d'Este, Sorita, Wicca Magickal Beginnings, Avalonia, 2008.

Rankine, David; d'Este, Sorita, Practical Elemental Magick, Avalonia, 2008

Redman, Graham, The Worshipful Master's Work Today (Emulation Pocket), Lewis Masonic, 2011.

Redman, Graham, The Warden's Work Today: With Notes for the Master Elect (Emulation Pocket), Lewis Masonic, 2011.

Redman, Graham, The Installing Master's Work Today: With Notes for the Immediate Past Master (Emulation Pocket), Lewis Masonic, 2011.

Rees, Julian, Tracing Boards of Three Degrees in Craft Freemasonry Explained, Lewis Masonic, 2009.

Rees, Julian, Ornaments Furniture and Jewels, Lewis Masonic, 2013.

Shah, Idries, The Sufis, Jonathan Cape, 1971.

Sinclair, Cornelius, The Walking Charge and other Masonic Performance Pieces, Seven Liberal Arts Press, 2014.

Smith, Rick, Learning Masonic Ritual - The Simple, Systematic and Successful Way to Master The Work [Kindle Edition], Rick Smith, 2013.

Smith, Rick, Learning Royal Arch Chapter Ritual - The Simple, Systematic and Successful Way to Master the Work [Kindle Edition], Rick Smith, 2014.

Steinmetz, George H, The Royal Arch: Its Hidden Meaning, Macoy Pub & Masonic Supply Co, 1979.

Symonds, John, & Grant, Kenneth, Confessions Of Aleister Crowley: An Autobiography by Aleister Crowley, Arkana books, (1989).

Tapsell, Jonathan, Ameth: The Life and Times of Doreen Valiente, Avalonia, 2014.

University of Bradford Web of Hiram http://www.brad.ac.uk/webofhiram/

Ward, Richard, Last of the Essex Cunning Men, Cauldron magazine No 152, May 2014 and No 154, Autumn 2014.

West, David, The Goat, the Devil and the Freemason, Hamilton House Publishing Ltd, 2013.

Williams Gareth; Pentz, Peter; Wemhoff, Matthias; Vikings: life and legend, British Museum Press, 2014.

Yates, Frances, The Rosicrucian Enlightenment, Paladin, 1975.

Zarcone, Thierry Professor. Gnostic/Sufi Symbols and Ideas in Turkish & Persian Freemasonry and in Masonic-Inspired Organisations, the Canterbury papers Vol 5, Knowledge of the heart: Gnostic Movements and Secret Traditions, Lewis Masonic, 2006.

INDEX

Published by Avalonia

www.avaloniabooks.co.uk

Milton Keynes UK
Ingram Content Group UK Ltd.
UKHW011416110424
440997UK00041B/245